Comedy, Tragedy, and Religion

Comedy, Tragedy, and Religion

JOHN MORREALL

STATE UNIVERSITY OF NEW YORK PRESS

Published by
State University of New York Press, Albany

For information, address State University of New York Press,
State University Plaza, Albany, N.Y., 12246

Production by Marilyn P. Semerad
Marketing by Anne M. Valentine

Library of Congress Cataloging in Publication Data

Morreall, John, 1947–
    Comedy, tragedy, and religion / John Morreall.
        p.   cm.
    Includes bibliographical references and index.
    ISBN 0–7914–4205–5 (hardcover : alk. paper). —
ISBN 0–7914–4206–3 (pbk. : alk. paper)
        1. Religions—Miscellanea.   2. Tragic, The—Religious aspects.
    3. Comic, The—Religious aspects.   I. Title.
    BL85.M72   1999
    200—dc21   98–51495
                                                                                CIP

10   9   8   7   6   5   4   3   2   1

*For
Jacob Neusner
who has opened
so many doors*

Contents

Acknowledgments

I am grateful to Victor Raskin, Editor of *Humor: International Journal of Humor Research*, for permission to reprint sections of my article "The Comic and Tragic Visions of Life," which originally appeared in *Humor* 11 (1998), 333–55.

Introduction

Human life is strange. We are here for a short time, involuntarily, uninvited, and with no explanation.
—Einstein, *The World as I See It*

God gives nuts to the toothless.
—Spanish proverb

If God lived on earth, people would break His windows.
—Yiddish proverb

*A*re these sayings comic or tragic? Both? Neither? Why do the central concerns of religion, such as death, show up so often in comedy? And why do discussions of tragedy so easily become religious discussions? Is there some special affinity between both tragedy and comedy, and religion? What makes religions such as Calvinism seem more tragic and less comic than, say, Zen Buddhism?

Many scholars have grappled with questions like these, but their answers have often appeared to contradict one another. Several books have traced the similarities between the Book of Job and Greek tragedy, for example, but other books count Job as a comedy.[1] W. H. Auden[2], Roy Battenhouse,[3] and others have written about Christian tragedy. Miguel de Unamuno even said that Christianity

1

embodies the tragic sense of life.[4] Karl Jaspers,[5] George
Skinner,[6] and D. D. Raphael,[7] on the other hand, have argued
that the very idea of Christian tragedy is incoherent.
Kierkegaard, whose own version of Christianity is often
treated as a paradigm of the tragic vision of life, said that "the
humorous is present throughout Christianity," indeed, that
Christianity is the most humorous view of life in world history.[8] And while St. Ambrose, John Chrysostom, and several
Protestant divines preached that comedy is inimical to
Christianity, and the Puritans outlawed comedy when they
ruled England, Harvey Cox and Conrad Hyers have claimed
that the comic vision is fundamental to Christianity.
Reinhold Niebuhr took an intermediate position. The comic
spirit, he wrote, is a "prelude" to faith, although it is inappro-
priate to allow it into any important area of human life.[9]

One problem with many claims made about tragedy,
comedy, and religion is that they are exaggerated. John
Wheelock, for example, wrote that tragedy "has been the
underlying theme in the work of every poet from Homer to
Eliot. It is implicit in any poet's vision of reality."[10] Another
problem is a lack of clarity. Nathan Scott's claim that comedy
embodies "the narrow escape into faith,"[11] for instance, has
rhetorical flourish but little clear meaning.

As long as terms are used without precision, and arguments are not carefully formulated, discussions of the relation of tragedy and comedy to religion can go on endlessly,
reaching no solid conclusions. What I would like to add to the
discussion is some precision and careful analysis, which will,
I hope, help to answer some basic questions, show the reason-
ableness of some positions and the unreasonableness of others, and show the relevance of tragedy and comedy to religion.

Chapter 1 lays out some basic connections between
tragedy, comedy, and religion. Chapters 2 and 3 explore the
nature of tragedy and the nature of comedy, chapter 4, what
makes their visions of life different. I argue that tragedy and
comedy involve contrasting ways of processing and evaluating human experience. Having clarified these visions of life,
we can then look for them in various religions. That is done in
chapters 5 through 9.

Chapter 1

Some Basic Connections

*C*omedy, tragedy, and religion have been intertwined from the beginning. In ancient Greece, tragedy and comedy emerged out of religious rituals—fertility cults in honor of Dionysus, a god who dies and is reborn each year. As these rituals moved into the cities and became civic drama, tragedies and comedies were performed together; in Athens, tragedies were presented in the morning and comedies in the afternoon. The great dramatists wrote both tragedies and comedies.

Some satyr plays, an early form of comedy, burlesqued traditionally serious characters, even characters from the tragedies with which the satyr plays were performed, as in Sophocles' *Ichneutai*. With a change from the tragic to the comic mask, the tragic hero became comic.

Much literary criticism in the last few centuries has belittled comedy in comparison with tragedy. Tragedy is "serious" drama, comedy "light" drama. When comedy occurs within tragedy, such as the drunken porter scene in *Macbeth*, it is usually labeled "comic relief." But the ancient Greeks, Shakespeare, and other dramatists took their comedy more seriously than that. They realized that comedy is not "time out" from the world; rather it provides another perspective on the world, a perspective no less true than the tragic perspective. As Conrad Hyers has suggested, comedy expresses a "stubborn refusal to give tragedy and fate the final say."[1]

For the Greeks, as for Shakespeare, the world presented in comedy was the same world presented in tragedy, and no subject was off-limits to comedy, not even the gods. The first fully developed comedy we have, Aristophanes' *The Acharnians*, has the demigod Amphitheus, the same sort of heroic figure found in tragedy, on a mission from the gods to arrange a peace between Athens and Sparta. But he has a problem: he's short of travel money and has to borrow from humans. In Aristophanes' *The Frogs*, the demigod Dionysus, on a journey to Hades, has to pay for his passage like anybody else, and must even help row the boat across the infernal lake, and that makes his backside sore. When scared at Pluto's gate, he soils himself. Later he is horsewhipped to test his claim of divinity. (Real gods don't cry.)

Not only do tragedy and comedy look at the same world, but they both tend to focus on its problematic side. Here again they connect with religion, which also focuses on the problematic side of human experience. Something can be problematic conceptually, or practically, or both. That is, we can have trouble, either fitting something into our general picture of the world, or knowing how to act in some situation.

Most problems involve evils of some kind, such as ignorance, failure, suffering, and vice. A major function of any religion is to help people understand and deal with evil, which they do through explanations, advice, and commands. Buddhism got its start from the problem of suffering. With its doctrine of redemption, Christianity offered a response to the problem of sin.

The experience of evil, or of any problem, is of a disparity between the way things are and the way we think they should be. Reinhold Niebuhr used the term "incongruity" for this disparity. "Things 'happen' to us. We make our plans for a career, and sickness frustrates us. We plan our life, and war reduces all plans to chaos."[2] Now, Niebuhr was discussing incongruities that elicit religious faith, but sickness, frustration, irrationality, war, and other basic incongruities are found in tragedy and comedy as well as in religion. All three are ways of facing "the awful truth," to use the title of a film comedy from the 1930s.

It is because all three are concerned with the disparity between the way things are and the way they should be, that irony is important in all of them. Indeed, the same irony can be religious, tragic, or comic. Consider the ancient conceit that the best fate is not to be born. Job asks God "Why did you let me be born? Why couldn't I have stayed in the deep waters of the womb?" It would have been better, Job says, if he had been carried from the womb to the grave, as if he had never existed (10:18–19). The line from *Oedipus Rex* is: "Not to be born is the best fate. But, if someone is born, then the next best thing is that he return whence he came as quickly as he can." With slight changes in the wording, and some appropriate facial expressions, these lines could also fit into a comedy.

The ultimate incongruity, death, is central in tragedy, comedy, and religion. In commenting on the Zen story of the master Wan Nienyi Zenji, who, just before dying, climbed into the coffin and pulled the lid closed, R. H. Blyth comments that "Death is the great subject for laughter as it is for tears."[3] Suicide is common in tragedies, but is also found in the silent comedies of Harold Lloyd and Charlie Chaplin, as well as in more recent film comedies like *The End*.

While religions, tragedy, and comedy all focus on the incongruities in life, tragedy and comedy have different responses to incongruity, and these are important in their visions of life. There are many ways to respond when things do not happen as they should—puzzlement, wonder, resentment, rage, despair, amusement. Tragedy embodies certain emotions and attitudes toward incongruities, like anger and rebellion, while comedy embodies the opposite response of not getting overly concerned. As Walter Kerr says, "the characteristic comic ending to a bit or to a play is a shrug. This is the way things are: bad, and not so bad."[4] As we will see, comedy presents incongruities as something we can live with, indeed, something in which we can take a certain delight.

Such differences in attitude can be profound. Tragedy generally treats war, for example, as an occasion to show valor and dignity in suffering, while comedy from its earliest days has treated war as folly.

Now a religion may embody a tragic response to incongruities, a comic response, neither, or both. More generally, it may embody elements of the tragic vision or the comic vision of life. Once we have clarified the tragic and comic visions, we will be in a position to look for them in various religious traditions.

Chapter 2

❖❖

The Nature of Tragedy

In this chapter we will analyze tragedy as a dramatic form. In the next we will examine comedy as a contrasting form. Then in chapter 4, we will contrast the visions of life in tragedy and comedy.

Four Features of Tragedy

I propose four main features of tragedy: the hero, conflict, suffering, and response. We can examine these one at a time.

The Hero

In tragedy, humans are portrayed as complex, noble beings capable of great thoughts, emotions, and actions. Many of the heroes in Greek tragedy were descended from the gods. Some claimed one divine parent; a few like Prometheus were fully divine. Several of Shakespeare's heroes seem like gods. Marlowe's Dr. Faustus bargained for divine knowledge. Friedrich von Schlegel even said that it was "the distinctive aim of tragedy . . . to establish the claims of the mind to a divine origin."[1]

Tragedy presents the value of human beings through events and actions in the lives of individuals such as Oedipus, Antigone, and Lear. While these characters embody human nature and the human condition, they are not typical humans. As Aristotle said, tragic heroes are superior to the average human being.[2] They are what ethologists would call supernormal instances of the species—they have human traits in great degrees. For many critics, twentieth-century plays like Arthur Miller's *Death of a Salesman* are not tragedies because their central figures are just average people, not tragic heroes.

Since heroic greatness is shown in actions, tragic heroes, like those in epic and melodrama, are known for great actions. Prometheus brought the arts of civilization to the human race, Oedipus rescued Thebes from the Sphinx and then vowed to bring the murderer of King Laius to justice.

What the tragic hero is striving for is almost always something good. We can forget this if we are overly influenced by Christian interpretations of Aristotle's discussion of *hamartia*, the tragic flaw. Many Christian commentators have interpreted this element as a moral shortcoming for which the hero suffers. But treating tragedies as morality plays is not true to Aristotle or to the genre.

Aristotle mentioned the tragic flaw only once in the *Poetics*—as a dramatic device to trigger the hero's fall. He did not think of the flaw and the fall as sin and punishment. Suffering that is deserved, he said, is not tragic, and so in tragedy the misfortune "is brought upon him not by vice and depravity but by some error of judgment."[3] For Aristotle the flaw did not have to be moral—it could simply be ignorance or bad judgment. For this reason it is misleading to talk about the tragic hero's "guilt" as similar to guilt for sin.

The tragic flaw, furthermore, was not a necessary ingredient even in the Greek tragedies Aristotle knew. Antigone had no moral or intellectual flaw. She is simply caught between two incompatible duties—her civic duty to obey the laws of Creon and her familial duty to bury her brother. Similarly, in Aeschylus's *The Suppliants*, King Pelasgus of Argos is an innocent man who knows what might happen to him if he pursues either of two courses of action. The fifty daughters of Danaüs have come to Argos as refugees. If he grants them asylum, he risks war with the country they fled. If he does not grant them asylum, he offends the gods. His problem is that whatever he does, he brings disaster on himself and his country.

Conflict

In tragedy the world is not a unified system ruled by a god or karmic principle, nor is it a home in which humans are meant to feel comfortable. Rather it is a complex of conflicting systems where human beings live in the shadow of failure, suffering, and death.

Life is full of tension, struggle, and danger, and our success or failure often depends on chance factors that we do not understand.

In our conflicts, too, we cannot count on outside help, either human or divine. As individuals and as a race, we are on our own.

Some of the conflicts we face are moral, but many are not. Good against evil is not even the most important conflict in tragedy. As A. C. Bradley said, "the tragic conflict is not merely one of good with evil, but also, and more essentially, of good with good."[4] That is shown in the tragedies of Antigone and Pelasgus. Berdiaev said that "the greatest tragedy is suffering caused by good, not by evil, and consists in our being unable to justify life in terms of the distinction between good and evil."[5]

Now although conflicts are unavoidable in any human life, not everyone faces them honestly. Humans have many ways of backing away from conflicts, denying involvement in them, and deceiving themselves about their nature or their gravity. Tragic heroes, however, face conflicts squarely. And they stick to their principles, keeping to the course of action they decided on, regardless of what happens.

Suffering

What happens is that the hero suffers, and usually ends up dying. The hero's anguish is not deserved and does not lead to some greater good which redeems it. If at the end of a drama the hero can say, "Well, it all came out for the best. My suffering was worth it," then the drama is not tragedy.

Response

Despite the tendency of the news media to call every serious accident a tragedy, suffering by itself is not tragic. The pain of an animal is not tragic for the animal, nor is the helpless suffering of a baby, or even the unthinking suffering of an adult. Passive suffering may evoke feelings of pity, but pity by itself is the stuff of melodrama rather than tragedy. In tragedy the suffering prompts the hero to think about what is happening. Tragic heroes question their suffering, resist it, and through it assert and define themselves.

Suffering is the natural occasion for this self-affirmation and self-definition. When everything in life is humming along, our desires are quickly fulfilled, and all our plans work out, we tend not to notice ourselves and our relation to the world. Like the car that always runs perfectly, the life that goes smoothly is not examined. It is when things go wrong that we look under the hood, or think about who we are, what we are doing, and what we want out of life.

The Emotional Effect of Tragedy on the Audience

With this understanding of the features of tragedy, we can now examine the emotional effect of tragedy on the audience, which since Aristotle has been considered an essential part of tragedy. An audience incapable of feeling emotions—say a group of Vulcans (the race of Mr. Spock on *Star Trek*)—could watch a performance of *Oedipus* or *Hamlet*, but could not experience a tragedy.

In the experience of tragedy, the emotions of the audience are keyed to the emotions of the characters, most importantly to those of the hero. It is heroes' emotions such as bravery, pride, and anger that show us the features discussed above—their nobility, the intensity of their suffering and their resistance to it, and their transcendence of their fate. Through their emotions heroes show us that they are heroes, and the events in the drama take on tragic meaning. Emotionless characters, such as Vulcans, might live through the same events as Antigone or Hamlet, but their stories would not be tragedies. Nor could a character lacking the right kinds of emotions be a tragic hero: someone whose only emotion was annoyance, say, and who engaged in petty bickering, would lack tragic stature. Tragic heroes are passionate about major issues in their lives and in the human condition.

The emotions of the supporting characters toward the hero also show us the hero's tragic stature, how much the hero is suffering, and what that suffering means. They thereby cue the audience as to how we should feel toward the hero.

There are two kinds of emotions we feel in response to the hero. First, our emotions may match theirs: we feel what they are feeling—fear, horror, and so forth. We can call this feeling *with* the hero. Secondly, we may have emotions like pity and admiration that do not duplicate their emotions. We can call this feeling *for* the hero.

Emotions we feel with and feel for the hero are reactions to their noble suffering. By the end of the tragedy, they transcend that suffering, and they are wiser and nobler than at the beginning. So our feelings for them go beyond pity to admiration or awe. Indeed, our feelings for tragic heroes have often been described as an experience of the sublime, which is why tragedy is often ranked as the highest art form. In a lesser art like melodrama, the characters may suffer greatly, and we may feel sorry for them, but they do not transcend their suffering and their fate, and so even if they experience anguish, it is not sublime.

The audience's tragic emotions are not meant to be felt during the performance and then forgotten. A good tragedy, like any worthy literature, does not simply evoke certain emotions toward particular characters and events, and leave it at that. Rather, it offers those emotions as the right emotions to feel in comparable situations in real life. It offers those situations-cum-emotions as paradigms, and so teaches us how to handle situations of failure, suffering, and death in our own lives. We should react as tragic heroes reacted, and as we reacted to them in tragedies. Participating in a worthwhile drama of any kind, like reading literature, educates our emotions.[6] That is a big part of why children in all cultures are educated with stories and drama—to show them how to respond to various kinds of events in life.

Earlier I suggested that what links tragedy, comedy, and religion is their concern with incongruities in life. Tragedy responds to incongruities heroically—with bravery, resoluteness, pride, and anger. Tragedy recommends that we be emotionally engaged with incongruities and that we overcome them or solve them. In the face of evil or other disparity between the way things are and the way they should be, we should maintain our dignity and struggle, willingly suffering whatever comes from the conflict. In short, tragedy recommends that we take incongruities seriously, indeed that we take everything seriously. In this respect and in others, as we'll see, tragedy is diametrically opposed to comedy.

Chapter 3

❖❖❖

The Nature of Comedy

*H*aving seen the basic features of tragedy, we are now in a position to compare them with comedy's basic features. I will concentrate on comedy as a kind of drama here, but most of what I say also applies to comic storytelling, songs, essays, films, monologues, and so forth. In literary criticism there are often distinctions between comedy, satire, farce, burlesque, and parody, but such distinctions will not figure into our analysis—I will use "comedy" to cover all of the above.

Literary critics and scholars of religion have analyzed comedy in a number of ways. J. Cheryl Exum and J. William Whedbee, for example. cite the "U-shaped" plot of certain books of the Old Testament—the way these stories move from social integration to social conflict to a new, realigned social structure, along with comic character types and dramatic forms like irony—to argue that these books are comic.[1] Although certain plot structures, character types, and dramatic forms are found in some comedy, however, they are not found in all comedy. More importantly, they do not pinpoint the essence of comedy—which is to make us laugh. While this connection between comedy and laughter may seem obvious, many scholars omit it from their analyses. Exum says that "At the outset one should dismiss the popular notion of comedy as something 'funny.' " On the contrary, I will argue, it is precisely in humor that we find the core of comedy.

Four Features of Comedy

A useful way to analyze comedy is to compare it with tragedy on the four features examined earlier.

The Hero

The most basic difference between comedy and tragedy lies in its central characters, who are not heroes, and often, as with Shakespeare's Falstaff, are antiheroic. Throughout comedy, the emphasis is on human limitations rather than human greatness. Even when comic characters defeat an opponent, it is seldom through strength or courage, and often through cleverness, which in comedy always beats raw power.

Both tragedy and comedy deal with incongruities like mistaken identities, misinterpreted messages, absurd coincidences, sickness, misfortune, suffering, and death. But comedy concentrates on the incongruities in human beings, especially their shortcomings. From its earliest days it has highlighted human ugliness, ignorance, folly, and vice; and its stock characters have been the hunchback, the fool, the windbag, the drunkard, the impostor, the hypocrite, and so forth.

A big part of the experience of comedy is laughing at these characters, who are traditionally called "comic butts." In the TV sitcom *M*A*S*H*, for example, Major Frank Burns was a selfish, childish, sneaky prig, and the laughter around him was usually at his inadequacies.

But besides these comic butts, most comedies have at least one character we laugh *with*. In *M*A*S*H* this was Lieut. Hawkeye Pierce, through whose eyes we saw characters such as Frank Burns. While comic butts are not recommended to the audience as role models, these characters are, like tragic heroes, paradigms for how to respond to incongruities.

"Comic hero" is the term most often used for these characters, but it is misleading, for they are not heroic. Indeed, many of them are proud of their weaknesses—Sir John Falstaff in Shakespeare's *Henry IV* is a cowardly liar with a fondness for overeating and getting drunk. For want of a better term, I will call these characters "comic protagonists."

Unlike the tragic hero, who strives for something great, the comic protagonist is typically striving merely to get along and have a good time. A comic protagonist who acquired noble, high-minded aspirations, indeed, would to that extent become less comic. As Nathan Scott said of Falstaff, he "simply lives for the joy of the adventure itself. . . . He has no quarrel with life: he is not a romantic; he is engaged in no cosmic debate: he is content simply to be a man."[2]

Conflict

In comedy, as in tragedy, the world is full of incongruities. Even more than the tragic world, the comic world is a hodge-podge of unsynchronized systems. Life is full of conflict, struggle, and danger, and success or failure often depends on unknown factors. Like tragic heroes, comic protagonists live in a world of failure, suffering, and death, and there is no special force looking out for them. But somehow, unlike tragic characters, they are at home in this world.

Suffering

In comedy conflict leads to suffering, but not to death, as often happens in tragedy. In comedy, the protagonist usually figures a way out of the conflict, and the suffering ends.

Response

Tragic heroes, as we saw, respond to conflict and the suffering it brings, in a confrontational way, with self-assertion and resistance. Comic protagonists, by contrast, usually handle conflicts and suffering with clever, indirect methods rather than confrontation. Instead of protesting or bemoaning their fate, they use their imagination to get out of trouble. They rely on their wits rather than weapons or willpower, and they are not given to emotions like resentment, self-pity, and sadness, which hamper creative thinking. Indeed, what distinguishes comedy from tragedy is largely the absence of emotions in comedy.

Humor versus Tragic Emotions

What is it to laugh at something, to see it as humorous? While there have been dozens of answers to these questions over the last two thousand years, I want to cite only the theory most widely accepted today, the Incongruity Theory. In its most general form, this theory says that laughing at something is enjoying some incongruity in it.

There have been many versions of the Incongruity Theory, and they have used different terminology.[3] "Incongruity" is what Reinhold Niebuhr and most psychologists call it, but Peter Berger uses "discrepancy,"[4] and Kierkegaard "contradiction."[5]

Common kinds of incongruity in comedy are human shortcomings such as ugliness, ignorance, folly, and vice. These are so common that from Plato on, critics of comedy have charged that comedy immerses us in human shortcomings, so that either they rub off on us, or we feel superior to our inadequate fellow humans.

But not all laughter is focused on shortcomings. Some is focused on skill or cleverness, as in the silent movies where Charlie Chaplin or Buster Keaton narrowly escapes death with an acrobatic stunt. Amusement at a surprising juxtaposition of ideas also need not involve feelings of superiority. I once took a three-year-old to a carnival where she spotted a cotton-candy vendor. "I want some," she said. "Some *what*?" I asked. "Ice cream fur," she answered. I laughed, not from feelings of superiority, but from delight at the liveliness of her imagination, which in an adult would be called "wit."[6]

To enjoy incongruity—in people's shortcoming, in their skill or cleverness, in their imagination, or whatever—is to enjoy a violation of our normal conceptual patterns and our expectations, and this requires a lack of practical concern, an emotional disengagement from what is here, now, real, and practical. If it is important to us that events meet our expectations, then experiencing incongruity will make us feel anxious, afraid, angry, or sad rather than amused. Only people who are open to things not going their way, are able to enjoy incongruity.[7] This is obvious when the incongruity is our own failure or misfortune. To laugh when we squirt the mustard past the hot dog onto our sleeve, for example, we have to escape self-centeredness and practicality. If we are concerned about how we look, and about getting lunch eaten, then we will be upset rather than amused. But laughter at other people also requires a suspension of concern. To laugh at the failure or misfortune of a friend or of a movie character, we have to suspend pity. As Henri Bergson put it, laughter requires a "momentary anesthesia of the heart."[8]

Another way to explain the practical unconcern and emotional disengagement in humor is to say that when we are laughing at something, we are in a playful, rather than a serious frame of mind. Practical concern and emotions like fear, anger, pity, and sadness involve seriousness; playfulness is the opposite of seriousness.

Humor's suspension of practical concern and emotions, and its playfulness are not limited to minor misfortunes. Some of the best humor comes out of catastrophes. After a tornado in the Midwest, a car that had been crushed by falling trees sported a handpainted sign: "COMPACT CAR." A newspaper photographer touring the Santa Barbara neighborhoods leveled by fire in 1988 found this sign on the smoking ruins of one house: "MY CHIMNEY'S BIGGER THAN YOURS."

Death, the ultimate catastrophe, is the subject of many jokes. When Thomas More was being led to the gallows for disagreeing with King Henry VIII, his arthritis made walking difficult. Approaching the scaffold, he asked the executioner, "Would you mind helping me up? I'll be able to get down by myself." Whole books have been written on humor in cemeteries.[9] One inscription on a gravestone in colonial Massachusetts reads "I told you I was sick." Another in New Orleans: "This is what I expected, but not so soon." Dorothy Parker's says simply: "Excuse my dust."

Comic protagonists show this kind of playfulness in the way they handle problems. Their attitude is the opposite of the self-absorbed emotions of tragic heroes. When they fail or experience misfortune, they are not steeped in self-pity, bemoaning their fate. Nor do they berate themselves with self-blame or regret. Instead they laugh off their difficulties, and get on with their lives.

The Effect of Comedy on the Audience

In tragedy, as we saw, the goal is to make us feel tragic emotions with and for the hero. In comedy the goal is to make us laugh with and at the protagonist, and at the comic butts. Humorless people could not experience comedy any more than emotionless people could experience tragedy.

Laughing at a situation, as we have seen, involves a lack of practical concern about its incongruity. When comic protagonists show this lack of concern, we share it with them and laugh. At other times we may be emotionally disengaged when they are serious, so that we laugh when they do not. Comedies are written to allow us a certain mental distance from the characters and their problems. Movies and cartoons, for example, often use unrealistic exaggeration to emphasize the fictional nature of what is happening.

However we achieve our mental distance, suspension of practical concern, and playfulness, these allow us to transcend the incongruities in the comedy to laugh at them. And as with tragedy, our reactions to what happens in comedy carry over to real life. Comedy encourages an emotional disengagement not only from the protagonist's problems, but from our own, and from the problems of the whole human race. We are liberated from ordinary concerns about what is here and now and real and practical, so that we may laugh at our own situations and at the human condition. As emotions like fear, anger, pity, sadness, and admiration are tragic paradigms for responding to real-life incongruities, so playfulness and laughter are comic paradigms for responding to real-life incongruities.

A good example of the comic spirit carried over to life emerged a few years ago when it was announced that astronomers had discovered an asteroid that will eventually crash into either Earth, the Moon, or Mars. If it crashed into Earth, it would hit with the force of a 20,000-megaton hydrogen bomb. Although this threat is real and the catastrophe could be the worst ever experienced by the human race, many newspapers reported the story with humor, as if it were the plot of a funny movie. One newspaper titled its editorial "The best protection: Root for Mars."

Examples like this give the lie to the common misconception that comedy is optimistic, as if it predicted a better future for the human race than tragedy does. While comic plots typically have a happy ending, they can involve just as much misfortune and hardship as tragedies. Comedy writers, as a group, are pessimistic. Think of Mark Twain, Dorothy Parker, and Woody Allen. The happy endings they sometimes put into their stories are just a dramatic convention, as we can see from the arbitrary, deus-ex-machina quality of many of those endings. When comic plots are allowed to take a natural course, they can end in catastrophe. The last scene in the film comedy *Dr. Strangelove*, for example, is a Cold War–era Air Force officer riding a nuclear bomb as it drops from a B-52 on its way toward Russia, starting World War III and perhaps ending the human race.

Walter Kerr offers this trenchant insight into the comic "happy ending":

> Compromise, resignation, doubt, frank disbelief on all sides, the denial of dignity, the reminder that victory changes nothing and that the bumbler will go on bumbling—these are the indispensable ingredients of a comic "happy" ending. . . . To be comic, the ending must forcefully call into question the issues of "happiness" and "forever after." Comedy is not lyric, not rhapsodic, not reassuring; putting its last and best foot forward, it puts it squarely down in dung.[10]

Comedy and tragedy do not predict different futures for their characters, then, or for the human race. They are based not on different kinds of events, but on different attitudes towards the same events. They embody different visions of the human condition.

Chapter 4

The Tragic Vision versus the Comic Vision

*T*ragedy and comedy, as we have seen, are not merely stories about fictional or historical characters. Dramatic
characters and the situations they face are representative of
human life in general, and the emotions they evoke from us
are the emotions recommended by drama as appropriate for
similar situations in life. Tragedy and comedy, in short,
embody visions of life.

A vision of life is a set of beliefs and attitudes. Just as
both a tragedy and a comedy can be written about the same
event, the tragic vision and the comic vision share many
beliefs. The most basic belief they share is that life is full of
incongruities, discrepancies between the way things ought to
be and the way they are. The difference between the two
visions of life is more in their attitudes than in any beliefs
about matters of fact. They involve different and usually
opposite ways of evaluating the same human condition.

In contrasting the tragic vision and the comic vision, we
can begin with differences in their cognitive psychology, and
then consider their social differences.

The Cognitive Psychology of the Tragic and Comic Visions: Mental Rigidity versus Mental Flexibility

The cognitive differences between the tragic and the comic
visions are deep and systematic. The most general contrast

can be called mental rigidity versus mental flexibility. These terms cover several contrasts, which we can discuss and relate to one another.

1. Simple versus Complex Conceptual Schemes

Tragic heroes approach life with relatively simple concepts that they want to apply neatly to every experience. In facing and working through a problem, the tragic hero tends to classify things and situations into opposites such as good and bad, and honorable and dishonorable, using straightforward criteria. This kind of thinking often turns problems into dilemmas unnecessarily, as only disastrous alternatives are envisaged, when in reality there are more possibilities. Sophocles' character Antigone, for example, thinks she must either obey Creon's decree not to bury her brother, or publicly violate the decree and suffer punishment. But in the same spot, a comic protagonist, or even an average politician, would see other possibilities. She might pick up her brother's body under cover of darkness, for example, and take it away to secretly bury it. She might stage a fire near the body and snatch it away in the confusion, creating the impression that it was destroyed in the fire. To anyone familiar with Greek tragedy, of course, these suggestions sound preposterous, but that is only because we have accepted the tragic mindset in which Antigone has only two choices.

In contrast to the rigidity of tragic thinking, comic thinking is flexible. Its protagonists do not approach life with simple concepts and narrow category systems into which every experience has to fit. They have more complex, messier sets of concepts that apply here but not there, today but not yesterday, and who knows about tomorrow?

The flexible thinking in comedy matches the complexity, diversity and movement of life itself. This flexibility shows especially in the twists and turns of its humor. As Suzanne Langer wrote, "the pure sense of life is the underlying feeling of comedy, developed in countless different ways. . . . The sense of life is always new, infinitely complex, therefore infinitely variable in its possible expressions."[1]

2. Low versus High Tolerance for Disorder

In the tragic vision there is a craving for order. This shows in tragedy's need for closure. Processes, once begun, have to be completed. Oedipus cannot rest until the murderer of Laius is found, even though, of course, he is that murderer.

Comedy, by contrast, is based on enjoying incongruity and so presents disorder as something we can live with, and even take delight in. From the earliest days of drama, comic plots have been messier than tragic plots. In a typical comedy by Aristophanes, for example, a theme is established in the first half, but the second half is merely comic "bits" improvised on that theme.

Comedies, too, have more characters than tragedies, and those characters are more diverse and unusual. Comedy does not require closure—it can live with loose ends and unanswered questions. Any play has to end somewhere, of course, and there is the tradition that comedies end on an upbeat note. But "happy endings" in comedy are famous for their arbitrariness and unnaturalness. They seldom constitute true closure.[2]

In commenting on Suzanne Langer's account of comedy, George Aichele has written that "there is nothing final about comedy . . . neither defeat nor victory. There is simply the ongoing movement, the series of battles and encounters, the capriciousness of Fortune, the processes of life."[3]

Unlike the linear, step-by-step thinking of tragedy, comic thinking is often wild. Comedy encourages "reframing," looking at situations from new and unusual perspectives. In many comedies, indeed, a half-dozen characters may each have their own understanding of a situation.

3. Preference for the Familiar versus Seeking Out the Unfamiliar

Tragic heroes prefer the physically and cognitively safe—the familiar, normal, routine, or standard. Unanticipated and unfamiliar events are threatening. Tragedy has a low tolerance for cognitive dissonance—for something that does not fit what we already know or believe. Tragic events violate those preferences, of course, and then the hero usually tries to bring things back to the way they used to be. Comedy, by contrast, being based on the enjoyment of incongruity, seeks out cognitive dissonance. What is strange and new represents not a threat but an opportunity.[4]

4. Low versus High Tolerance for Ambiguity

In the tragic vision there is a desire for things and events to fit neatly into categories. Ambiguity is shunned: everything should be clear and have one meaning.[5] Tragedy goes for *the* truth about each thing and situation, and for absolute truth rather than relative truth.

Comedy, by contrast, is not put off by ambiguity and multiple meanings. In fact, it uses them regularly—without them there could be no jokes, for instance.[6] And in comedy there is no obsession with reaching the absolute truth about anything, if that notion even makes sense in comedy. Harvey Cox has written that wherever we "live at the vortex of multiple worlds of meaning, the comic is possible. Only in a closed, monolithic universe is it excluded."[7]

Ambiguity is important in characters, too, as Conrad Hyers has argued. "Comedy mixes and confounds all rigid categories and fixed identities," as in Charlie Chaplin's Little Tramp, at once an aristocrat and a bum. Clowns generally are mixtures. Comic protagonists may be good, but ambiguously so—consider Shakespeare's character Falstaff or the cartoon character Bugs Bunny. "The comic virtues, from laughter to love, are made possible because they embody a greater appreciation for the muddiness of human nature and the ambiguities of human truth and goodness."[8]

5. Convergent versus Divergent Thinking

The drive in tragedy for reaching "the truth" puts the emphasis on what is past, and more generally, on what is real. The tragic mind is the left-brain, information-processing intellect, the mind at work. In comedy, the imagination, the mind at play, is as important as the intellect. While there is no such thing as tragic fantasy, there are comedies such as Shakespeare's *A Midsummer Night's Dream* which are all fantasy.

Most thinking in tragedy is what psychologists call convergent thinking—trying to find the single correct answer to a problem, as in mathematical computation. In this mode there is no room for making unusual connections between ideas. In comedy a different kind of thinking comes into play—divergent thinking, thinking in which there is no single correct answer, where unusual relationships and analogies are explored, and no train of thought is out of bounds. Divergent thinking need not be aimed at answers, but when it is, it looks for many answers rather than one. Consider these two standard exercises in divergent thinking:

— Make a list of thirty uses for a brick.
— Make a list of thirty improvements on the standard bathtub/shower—money is no object.

6. Uncritical versus Critical Thinking

Because tragic heroes think in standard ways and because they seek familiar order, they tend not to call into question the categories and patterns of thought that they inherit. Comic protagonists, on the other hand, and the whole practice of comedy, point out incongruities; in language, in people's reasoning, and more generally, in the established order of things. Aristophanes poked fun at political leaders, at intellectual figures like Socrates, even at the gods; and from then to today's stand-up comedians and *The Simpsons*, the comic spirit has been the critical spirit.

7. Emotional Engagement versus Emotional Disengagement

One reason why tragic heroes show little creativity and critical thinking is that they respond to challenges with emotions. Whether considered positive, like pride, or negative, like fear and sadness, emotions lock heroes into self-concern and into their own perspectives, just as they do to us in real life. In emotional states, we tend to act in automatic, habitual, less intelligent ways; and the stronger the emotion, the less rational our actions. That is why rage and even love are called "blind." Strong emotions tend to magnify the situation at hand, and block rational thinking that would put things into perspective. Tragic heroes, driven by emotions, tend to be extremists: to reach the goal set by their emotions, they will sacrifice everything else, including their own lives and the lives of those they love. Oedipus presses his search for Laius' killer even though he has been warned of the dire consequences. Hamlet will prove the King's guilt and try to execute perfect justice, no matter what it costs him and those around him. Ahab will kill Moby Dick or die trying.[9]

Comic characters, by contrast, tend to keep an unemotional clearheadedness even in extreme situations. Confronted by misfortune, they do not sink into self-pity or shake their fists at the sky—futile responses that at best would make them feel good for a moment. They think rather than feel their way through the problem, engaging their imagination and ingenuity instead of their emotions. They are adaptable, surviving by their wits and their wit. ("Wit" originally meant all mental abilities.) This emotional disengagement gives comic characters perspective and objectivity in handling problems, allowing them to laugh amid misfortune—something tragic heroes never do.

Now, there is a certain satisfaction in feeling tragic emotions like self-pity and indignation, and experiencing these feelings vicariously is a big part of the audience's satisfaction in tragedy. These emotions make possible our admiration of the tragic hero as sublime. But, however satisfying tragic emotions may be, they make tragic characters, and vicariously the audience, mentally rigid, even obsessive. That rigidity makes the characters less adapted to their situations; and to the extent that we imitate them in our own lives, it makes us less adapted to handling our problems.

Faced with some problem, then, the tragic response is to be fully engaged with it, while the comic response is to step back and see it as part of the big picture. When put into perspective, most of life's hardships are less hard, and many are downright funny. With comic vision, not only are we better able to handle the problem, but we often find elements of delight in it. So comic protagonists are more likely to enjoy experiences of all kinds, and to the extent that we imitate them, we are too.

Many problems cannot be solved, of course, as tragedy constantly reminds us. With them, the best we can do is cope, and here too disengagement has much to recommend it. A contemporary example of comic perspective is the humorist writer Erma Bombeck. A few years ago she wrote a book about children with cancer: *I Want to Grow Hair, I Want to Grow Up, I Want to Go to Boise,* her title pieced together from essays by the kids. After writing it, Bombeck was herself diagnosed with breast cancer, which required a mastectomy. In that situation many women would have reacted with tragic emotions, but not Bombeck.

> I thought of the thousands of luncheons and dinners I had attended where they slapped a name tag on my left bosom. I always smiled and said "Now, what shall we name the other one?" That would no longer be a problem.[10]

Here is rationality triumphing over emotions. As Horace Walpole said, the world is a comedy to those who think, a tragedy to those who feel.

8. Stubbornness versus Willingness to Change One's Mind

The mental rigidity of tragic heroes shows not only in their thinking and in their emotions, but in their decision making. Once they choose a course of action, they tend to stick to it no matter what happens. Early in the history of tragedy, Sophocles had already perfected what Walter Kerr calls "the tragedy of the locked will," most familiar in Oedipus's relentless search for the murderer of Laius, and in Antigone's and Creon's unwillingness to budge from their initial positions. The downfall of such characters is made inevitable as much by their locked wills as by any external force.[11]

Tragic heroes themselves, of course, see their stubbornness as single-mindedness, commitment, whole-heartedness, devotion to duty, resoluteness of purpose, or some other virtue. They would have a hard time understanding Bertrand Russell's little conjugation: "I am firm, you are stubborn, he is pig-headed."

Like tragic heroes, comic protagonists make decisions, but they are adaptable after setting a course of action. As situations change, they can too, so that when a new opportunity arises, they can take advantage of it. They have not even determined once and for all what will count as success or failure.

Because of this flexibility, their plans and actions are more contingent than those of tragic heroes. This contingency is mirrored in the contingency of events in comedy. While tragedy emphasizes the inevitable, comedy emphasizes fortune and serendipity. The whole spirit of comedy, said Suzanne Langer, is "essentially contingent [and] episodic," while tragedy is "closed, final, and passional."[12]

To highlight the disadvantages of stubbornness and other forms of mental rigidity, comedy presents as comic butts the miser, the paranoid, the pedant, and other characters whose wills or intellects are in ruts. The idée fixe that dominates the tragic hero is in comedy something to laugh at. Indeed, Henri Bergson based his whole theory of comedy on characters with idées fixes, who represent what he called "mechanical inelasticity."[13]

9. Idealism versus Pragmatism

With its desire for simple unambiguous categories and conceptual order, the tragic vision is idealistic, in two senses. First, it prefers clean abstracta like Truth, Justice, and Duty to messy concreta—people, things, and situations. When tragedy shows its metaphysics, there is usually a tendency to Platonic realism. Secondly, the tragic vision craves an ideal, perfect world. Its heroes are driven by principles. Oedipus, Antigone, and Hamlet want perfect truth and justice. Othello wants his wife's faithfulness to be beyond any possible suspicion.

In the comic vision, on the other hand, there is no craving for abstractions or for absolutes. Indeed, characters with such cravings have been comic butts since Aristophanes poked fun at Socrates in *The Clouds*. The stuff of comedy is concrete things, people, and situations. From Falstaff to Charlie Chaplin's Little Tramp, comic protagonists are concerned not about truth and justice and duty, but about their next meal, paying the rent, and getting the one they love to love them. The art of writing comedy lies largely in handling physical details—think of the work of Mark Twain, Dorothy Parker, and Dave Barry.

Opposed to the idealism of the tragic vision is comic pragmatism. While tragedy longs for some utopia or heaven, and never finds our merely human lives worth living, the comic vision gets along fine in the everyday world. Unlike tragic heroes, comic characters are full of quirks, foibles, vices, and other limitations. In comedy happiness is not something to be found in a perfect world: it is something we cobble together here and now. At death what comic protagonists would ask for is not heaven, but simply more of the same. The comic vision would just not work in a world of angels or disembodied souls.

A good place to see this opposition between the idealism of tragedy and the pragmatism of comedy, is Christopher Fry's short play *A Phoenix Too Frequent*, which contrasts nicely with Shakespeare's *Romeo and Juliet*. Dynamene has recently lost her husband, and in her grief is about to kill herself at his grave. But a handsome soldier passes by. He is troubled too, for he was supposed to guard the corpses of six hanged men, and one of the corpses has been stolen. Unless he can get the number of the corpses back to six, he will be court-martialed and probably executed. Breaking out of her grief, Dynamene comes up with a solution: the soldier can have her husband's body as his sixth corpse, and the soldier's life will be spared. When he is shocked by this plan, she replies:

> How little you can understand. I loved
> His life not his death. And now we can give his death
> The power of life. Not horrible: wonderful!
> Isn't it so? That I should be able to feel
> He moves again in the world, accomplishing
> Our welfare? It's more than my grief could do.[14]

10. Finality versus a Second Chance

The corpse's ability to save the soldier's life here brings out another contrast between the tragic vision and the comic. In tragedy each action or event leads inexorably to certain consequences, so that once we make a mistake or misfortune strikes, our fate is sealed. In the comic vision, on the other hand, life is not so harsh, at least for the clever person. When we make a mistake, we can often correct it, or at least cover it up so that it will not harm us. Even with calamities, we may be able to improvise a way out.

11. Spirit versus Body

The idealism of the tragic vision shows clearly in its low opinion of the physical aspects of human life. Tragedy bemoans our messy, limited, embodied condition, and often dualistically identifies the human being with the mind, spirit, or soul. The aspirations of tragic heroes are for abstractions, not for something physical such as pleasure. Indeed, the more tragic they get, the more abstract they get, and the less they would even think of something like pleasure. While in the early part of *Romeo and Juliet,* young Romeo felt physically attracted to Juliet, Walter Kerr points out, as the play becomes a tragedy, "Romeo is no longer interested in sex . . . if he were interested in sex, he would not kill himself."[15]

Comedy, by contrast, embraces our bodily existence and physical needs like food and sex. Falstaff might deliver a monologue while gnawing on a leg of mutton: it is inconceivable that Hamlet would do so. While most tragedy could dispense with the body—angels have been tragic characters—the body has always been essential in comedy. Comedy celebrates our physical vitality and our delight in biological living. In the comic vision, the person who pretends to be above physical life has always been good for a joke, from Aristophanes' *The Clouds* to *New Yorker* cartoons poking fun at yogis and mystics.

Instead of mind/body dualism, comedy has always at least implicitly espoused monism. We are thinkers, to be sure, but we are also eaters, sleepers, lovers, and so forth. Consider the first comic image from the first comedy we have of Aristophanes, *The Acharnians*:

> Alone in the morning, here I take my place,
> Here I contemplate, here I stretch my legs;
> I think and think—I don't know what to think.

> I draw conclusions and comparisons,
> I ponder, I reflect, I pick my nose,
> I make a stink—I make a metaphor,
> I fidget about, and yawn and scratch myself.[16]

Nathan Scott even claims that "the major purpose of the comedian is to remind us of how deeply rooted we are in all the tangible things of this world."[17]

The physicality of our lives imposes limitations, of course; we cannot, like angels, achieve something by fiat. Most of our goals require work, and often we fail. But these facts call for patience and cleverness, not for resentment. Nor are the limitations of human life always negative; they can be pleasant in that they evoke help from other people. Young children get pleasure from being helped and comforted in their smallness and helplessness. As Walter Kerr puts all this, "We see that we are vulnerable. But we are also amused and happy to be vulnerable, because our vulnerability has brought us, even as infants, so many warm comforts. . . . Dependence so often ends in delight."[18]

While tragic heroes are never at home in this limited material world, comic protagonists are often comfortable here.

12. Seriousness versus Playfulness

The tragic vision of life is a paradigm of seriousness, and explaining the nature of seriousness explains a good deal about the tragic vision.

It is *persons*, I take it, who are serious in the basic sense of the word. Things like problems are called "serious" because they require persons to be serious about them.

For us to be serious is to be solemn and given to sustained, narrowly focused thought. It is also for us to be earnest, that is, sincere, in what we say and do. We say only what we believe, and act only according to our real intentions.

An issue is serious. as I said, if it calls for us to be serious—as we think about, talk about, and act on it. If the issue is a problem, it is an important problem, one that should rank high on our agenda, and one that may rightly make considerable demands on us. An issue is important, in short, if it commands our full and sustained attention.

Herein lies the connection so obvious in tragedy between seriousness and negative emotions. To be serious about an issue is to be concerned about events related to that issue. More specifically, it is to be concerned that things happen in accord with our values. If, as in tragedy, things do not go as we desire, then our concern becomes fear, anger, sadness, or other negative emotion. The serious person, then, is either in an emotional state, or is one event away from an emotion.

Seriousness is often contrasted with joking and humor, but the attitude opposite seriousness is actually wider than these. The closest word I can find for this attitude is "playfulness." When we are playful, we are not solemn and are not given to sustained, narrowly focused thought. Our thinking tends to be divergent rather than convergent. We are also not bound to earnestness in what we say and do. We may say something outlandishly false for the mental jolt it gives us and others. We may impersonate someone, or feign some emotion—as we might try on a Halloween costume—just for the fun of it. In general, we engage in playful communication and action for their own sake, not to reach or convey truth, or to achieve some other goal.

In contrasting seriousness with playfulness here, I am not denying that aspects of the two can coexist. What Martin Buber calls an "I-Thou" relationship, for example, can be engaged in for its own sake, and in that way resemble play, but at the same time can be momentous, and in that way resemble seriousness.

Now some people are serious only occasionally, or only about a few issues, while others are serious virtually all the time, about everything. A vision of life such as the tragic vision can be serious, when it evaluates most or all situations in life as serious, that is, as calling for our solemn, narrowly focused, resolute attention.

Unlike the tragic view, the comic view treats most events in life as nonserious—as not calling for our solemn, narrowly focused, resolute attention. It sees playfulness as appropriate in many or most situations.

We can be playful in several senses, each opposed to a sense of "serious." First we can be not-grave, not engaged in deep, narrowly focused thought. Secondly, we can be not-sincere in what we say and do. As a joke, we can engage in non–bona fide communication and activity. We can exaggerate, understate, or even deny what we believe to be true. We can treat inanimate objects as people, friends as enemies, and so forth—all for the fun of it.

These senses of "playful" and their corresponding senses of "serious" are connected with another distinction—the one between play and work. When we are serious, we are usually in a practical frame of mind in which we want to achieve some goal. We are working toward something, and anything playful would be a distraction. In play, on the other hand, we engage in some activity, not to get results, but simply for the pleasure of the activity itself. It is in this sense that we "play" rather than "work" music. The comic vision encourages us to treat most situations in life like music, as something to be played.

The Social Differences between the Tragic and Comic Visions

So far we have been exploring the cognitive differences between the tragic and comic views—the differences in the ways individuals understand and evaluate the experiences in their lives. But life is social as well as individual and any vision of life has a social dimension. Here, too, there are deep differences between the tragic vision and the comic.

13. Heroism versus Antiheroism

Many of the social differences between the two visions of life can be traced to the fact that the tragic vision is heroic, and the comic vision antiheroic. Tragedy, along with epic, define the heroic tradition in literature. Their central characters are superhuman, sometimes semidivine beings, larger-than-life, facing monumental struggles. Tragedy and epic have flourished in cultures that believed in heroes, and have declined in cultures like our own that do not.

The comic vision is antiheroic. Its characters are not larger-than-life in any respect except in their shortcomings. Comedy goes out of its way to expose authority figures for their pretenses to heroic stature, and it frequently parodies both tragedy and epic.

14. Militarism versus Pacifism

Tragedy and epic arose in warrior cultures and the tragic vision embodies warrior values. A hero, as the dictionary says, is a man known for courage and nobility, especially in war. Someone shows heroism in a battle or other struggle, and the virtues needed by the hero are those of a good soldier— strength, courage, devotion to duty, resoluteness of purpose, and commitment to a code of honor. Although there are a few antiwar tragedies like Euripides' *Trojan Women*, these military virtues are the basic values in the tragic vision.

The comic vision, by contrast, is antimilitarist, and often pacifist. From Aristophanes' play *Lysistrata*, about soldiers' wives holding a sex strike to stop the Peloponnesian War, to Stanley Kubrick's movie *Dr. Strangelove*, about the insanity of the Cold War, comedies have lampooned the willingness to kill or die on command. Comic protagonists are not willing to kill or die for much, if anything. They are usually good at talking their way out of conflicts, and when that fails, they are not ashamed to run away. The comic attitude here is captured in the old Irish saying "You're only a coward for a moment, but you're dead for the rest of your life." The mental rigidity praised in tragedy as courage or valor is seen in comedy as the irrational willingness to obey orders at tremendous cost to everyone involved. Tragic heroes preserve their dignity but die in the process; comic protagonists lose their dignity but live to tell the tale.

In the comic vision, as in the tragic, life is full of conflicts, but they are not to be handled by head-on confrontation. Violence is likely to make things worse. Instead of fighting opponents or evil forces, comic protagonists trick them, make peace with them, work around them, or escape them.

15. Vengeance versus Forgiveness

In the militarism of tragedy, an offense against a person has a finality that it lacks in comedy. Offending a tragic hero triggers a response of vengeance, which the hero is then locked into, usually until the offender or the hero is killed. In comedy, on the other hand, forgiveness is common. As Aristotle pointed out, in comedy enemies sometimes become friends, but never in tragedy.

16. Hierarchy versus Equality

Heroic and military ideologies are socially hierarchical, authoritarian, and elitist. A few people, the leaders, are important and deserve our respect; the rest of us, the followers, are not important. Tragic heroes come from the upper classes, usually from royalty, and the dialogue shows that. In ancient Greece tragic heroes were often of divine origin, even half-god or, like Prometheus, fully divine. Characters who are not nobles may have bit parts in tragedy, but the tragedy could never be about them.

The comic vision, by contrast, is egalitarian rather than elitist: everybody counts, and anyone may have an interesting part to play. Comedy has always valued what is now called "diversity," not only because it is egalitarian, but because it makes for more fun. Comic protagonists may come from any class. In ancient comedy slaves got laughs at the expense of their masters, and ever since comedy has championed the "little guy" and the "underdog"—Chaplin's Little Tramp, Shirley Temple, the secretaries in the movie *Nine to Five*, the boy beset by burglars in *Home Alone*, and so on. When socially high-ranked characters appear in comedy, they are often made fun of, especially if they "put on airs." And rather than the elevated language of tragedy, comedy uses common speech.

17. Less versus More Sexual Equality

Since heroic ideologies are male-dominated, it is natural that sexism is part of the tragic vision. In the antiheroic comic vision, there is more equality between the sexes. More comic characters are women, they have a wider variety of roles, and they often outwit men. By the time of Aristophanes' *Lysistrata*, comedy already had its theme of clever, nonviolent women outsmarting warriors. Indeed, such comedy may have been the first form of feminism in Western culture.

18. Respect for versus Questioning of Authority and Tradition

The contrast drawn earlier between uncritical tragic thinking and critical comic thinking has social consequences. The tragic vision, and the heroic tradition generally, emphasize respect for authority and tradition. That gives them much of their solemnity. Tragic heroes are almost never social critics or rebels, and when they are, they are usually upholding an older power structure against a newer one. Antigone, for example, upholds a family obligation against a state decree. (An exception here is Prometheus, but his rebellion was on behalf of the human race against the gods.)

In the comic vision, on the other hand, authority and tradition are questioned and tested rather than blindly accepted. Aristophanes poked fun at political leaders, philosophers, even the gods; and ever since, a good part of comedy has been social and political satire. The comic mind looks for inconsistencies, blunders, phoniness, and other incongruities, and authorities and traditions are a rich source of them. So comedy is naturally iconoclastic.

19. Rules versus Situation Ethics

Tragedy's emphasis on respect for authority and tradition, and its desire for clear decision procedures and, more generally, order, explain its emphasis on our duty to obey rules. By contrast, in comedy, there is little or no commitment to rules. Telling comic characters that they must do their duty is likely to raise a mocking salute and a snicker. That is why many critics of comedy have charged it with amorality, even anarchy.

Comic heroes may happen to follow a set of rules as long as they work, but they are unwilling to make a commitment to follow the rules no matter what. They refuse to decide how they will decide in the future, because unique situations may require unique responses. Like the "situation ethics" discussed in Christian circles a few decades ago, the comic vision is wary of exceptionless generalizations in morality or anywhere else.

20. Social Isolation versus Social Integration

In tragedy the spotlight is on an individual, usually a person who gets more socially isolated as the action progresses. Tragic plots involve social relations, but these tend to be the transactions of individuals following codes of conduct for dealing with other individuals.

The opposite is true in comedy, where the basic unit is the group, and the interactions of group members are not the formal relationships of tragedy, but the free-flowing, spontaneous relationships of friends. When a loner appears in comedy, it is as someone to be incorporated into the group. The person who refuses this integration—the hopeless egoist, snob, or miser—is a comic butt or a source of laughter.

The activity in comedy is not that of an individual, but of a family, a village—or in TV sitcoms, a bunch of coworkers, the patrons of a bar, and so forth. Presenting this action often involves several stories going on at the same time.

Problems in comedy must often be resolved by the group. A common theme is that one or more members have been separated from the others, or are threatened with separation, but then are brought safely back into the group.

Even when comedy presents problems of individuals, those characters do not go it alone, but get by with a little help from their friends. There is a striking contrast here with tragic heroes. Often what makes characters' suffering tragic is precisely that they respond to problems with self-concerned horror, anger, or self-pity, rather than turning to others for support.

Now, there is a certain satisfaction in such "Woe is me" emotions—we get to focus all our attention on ourselves and what is important to us. Standing alone against the world can produce powerful feelings of self-worth. Such emotions can make tragic heroes, and vicariously audiences, feel noble, valorous, even martyrlike. But tragic heroes easily go beyond self-reflection and self-esteem to self-obsession. They become isolated from others, who, after all, also suffer.

If tragic heroes shared their experience, Walter Kerr suggests, they might turn into comic characters. If on the way out of Thebes, Oedipus ran into another man who had killed his father and married his mother, "tragedy would be as swiftly dead. Let the two men compare notes, become cronies in corruption, and laughter must break loose no matter what has gone before."[19]

Earlier we commented that comic protagonists can mentally distance themselves from their problems so as to laugh. That mental distance has important social consequences. Humorist Will Rogers quipped that everything is funny if it happens to the other person. Comedian Mel Brooks said, "Tragedy is me cutting my finger; comedy is you falling down a manhole and dying." Stripped of hyperbole, the principle here is that laughing at a problem requires some emotional disengagement from it, as when it is someone else's problem. To laugh at our own problems we have to see ourselves from the outside rather than from a self-privileging perspective. In the words of the old *Candid Camera* jingle, we have to see ourselves "as other people do." Laughing at ourselves, then, requires that we see ourselves in social perspective, which is why people who can laugh at themselves get along well with others, while people who cannot laugh at themselves do not get along.

In comedy there is misfortune, war, and the other ills found in tragedy. But because the characters are all in it together, the experience is different. Hardships that would bring great suffering to isolated individuals are much easier for groups to cope with. As anyone knows who has been through hard times with close friends, when we are struggling together there is often a thin line between suffering and fun.

Tragedy, with its emphasis on the individual, treats death as the ultimate evil, the end of everything. However, when someone dies in comedy, life goes on because the group goes on, as is seen in comedy's standard endings—the wedding and the birth.

Conclusion: Individual Struggle or Social Adventure

The tragic and comic views, then, agree in their basic beliefs that life is full of incongruities—folly, disappointment, vice, mistakes, danger, and suffering—and that we humans are on our own in handling them. Whatever powers or forces may control the universe, they are doing little or nothing to guarantee our happiness.

Where the two views differ is in their attitudes toward these incongruities and toward life itself. In the tragic view we live as individuals. All activity is serious, and is usually done to accomplish something. Life is hard work. We struggle solemnly, emotionally engaged with everything that happens to us. In the end we are doomed to failure, but at least we can show heroism in the struggle.

In the comic view, we live as groups. Much of our activity is for its own sake, and much of that is not serious. We play as well as work. And even when we are trying to accomplish something, taking risks can bring delight, whether or not we meet our goal. The adventure is rewarding in itself. When we are striving for a goal, too, we should not be emotionally engaged by every negative event, for emotions often make us less able to cope with problems. Besides, it feels better to laugh than to cry.

The tragic vision embodies an attitude similar to the old motto: "It doesn't matter whether you win or lose. It's how you play the game." This motto also fits the comic vision, I would add, but what the two visions look for in the game is quite different. For the tragic view, in struggling through life's twists and turns, the best I can achieve is individual nobility or grandeur. For the comic view, which puts no stock in the sublime, the best we can achieve is adventure with friends: we can take delight in the many shifts of thought and fortune we go through. We can experience life as funny and fun.

Chapter 5

❖❖

The Tragic and the Comic Visions in Religions

*H*aving explored in detail the tragic and the comic visions of life, we are now in a position to consider them in relation to the world's religions. In the first chapter we traced some basic connections between religion and tragedy and comedy. Tragedy and comedy began as religious rituals, and like religions focus on the problematic side of life. All three are concerned with the incongruities of the human condition. That is why irony figures in all three—irony as a trope and as a feature of human experience. Like tragedy and comedy, religions are concerned with the conflict between the way things seem and the way they are. In philosophical Hinduism, for example, the whole of our ordinary experience is misleading; in reality all that exists is one unchanging Self. Buddhism denies this one unchanging self, but as part of its general denial that any selves exist. In the monotheistic religions, the world of selves and objects is real enough, but there is irony in the values we attach to this world—too often we place more importance on what is fleeting and trivial than on what is genuinely important.

Several religious texts have thematic similarities with tragedies. Buddha's central question was the central question in tragedy: how should human beings handle suffering and death? The Biblical story of Job is similar in several ways to that of Oedipus. Jesus' cry on the cross, "My God, my God, why have you forsaken me?" sounds tragic.

41

Comic themes also appear in religion. Conrad Hyers argues, for example, that the book of Jonah is a satire on a reluctant prophet,[1] an argument we will examine in chapter 7. In comedy and in most religions, the pursuit of worldly glory is foolish, the underdog or little guy is championed, and events that seem catastrophic turn out to be beneficial. Most generally, comedy and religion encourage a spirit of detachment from day-to-day concerns.

In looking for the comic and tragic visions in religions, then, we can look for comic and tragic themes, stories, and values. We can also look for comic and tragic role models. We can ask, for example, in what ways Moses, Jesus, or Buddha might embody the comic or tragic vision. Here, and generally, we can use the twenty contrasts between the tragic vision and the comic vision presented in the last chapter. No religion, we admit right off, will count as tragic or as comic by all twenty criteria; neither the tragic vision nor the comic vision is found in pure form in any religion. A religion might have only a few tragic features or a few comic features, and it might also have features of *both* the tragic and the comic visions.

As we examine each religion, we will be looking for features that show at least a tendency toward the tragic vision; these I call pro-tragic features. We will also be looking for pro-comic features, those that show at least a tendency toward the comic vision. As we saw in the last chapter, the tragic and the comic visions usually represent opposite tendencies, so that most pro-tragic features will at the same time be anti-comic features, and most pro-comic features will be anti-tragic features.

In calling certain features of religions pro- or anti-tragic, or pro- or anti-comic, I mean only that those features *incline* those religions toward or away from the tragic or the comic vision, not that their presence in a religion guarantees that it is tragic or comic. To take a parallel case from a nonreligious vision of life, Stoicism has important pro-comic features such as encouraging emotional distance and seeing things as part of the big picture, but at the same time Stoicism seems to lack a basic trait of comedy—finding humor in life's problems.

Pro-Tragic Features

In our contrast of the tragic and comic visions in the last chapter, we saw that both in its psychology of the individual and in its social psychology, the tragic vision involves a more rigidly structured approach to life than the comic vision. It countenances fewer possibilities and finds fewer sources of happiness in life. Specifically, we pointed out that in its psychology of the individual, the tragic vision tends toward:

1. Simple conceptual schemes
2. A low tolerance for disorder
3. A preference for the familiar
4. A low tolerance for ambiguity
5. Convergent thinking
6. Uncritical thinking
7. Emotional engagement with problems
8. Stubbornness
9. Idealism (metaphysical and moral)
10. A sense of finality—that we get just one chance at anything
11. An emphasis on spirit over body
12. Seriousness

In its social psychology, the tragic vision tends toward:

13. Heroism
14. Militarism
15. Vengeance
16. Hierarchy
17. Less sexual equality
18. Respect for authority and tradition
19. A concern with rules
20. Social isolation rather than social integration.

We derived these twenty features mostly from literary tragedies—stories of characters who were born once, lived, and died, and then their lives were over. But in looking for the tragic vision in religions, we must remember that most religions teach some kind of afterlife exists, either in heaven or hell, or, through reincarnation, in this world. If a religion teaches that human life goes on forever, then we have to examine the whole of that life, and not just the first part, for pro-tragic and anti-tragic features.

Some religions have obvious pro-tragic features and others have obvious anti-tragic features, but our full list of twenty criteria will not apply neatly to any religion, and so we will not attempt to explicitly rate each religion on each criterion. Instead, we will pick out the pro-tragic and anti-tragic features that stand out in the various religions.

We will also use five comprehensive questions, listed below with the answers of the tragic vision. These answers provide a Tragic Profile against which to compare religions.

1. *Is suffering orderly and so understandable, or is it random and not understandable?*
The tragic vision answers that at least some suffering is not understandable.

2. *Is suffering avoidable?*
The tragic answer is that suffering is not avoidable in many cases.

3. *Does suffering always at least have the potential to bring about some greater good—by building our character, serving as just punishment, warning us to change our lives, and so forth? Or is some suffering pointless?*
The tragic answer is that much suffering is pointless.

4. *Is there reason to hope that in the big picture and the long run, life will turn out happy—for the individual, for the group, or for the whole human race?*
The tragic answer to all these questions is No.

5. *How should we react to suffering?*
The tragic answer is "With noble resistance."

Pro-Comic Features

In looking for the comic vision in religions, we can use the other side of the twenty contrasts from chapter 4. Under the cognitive psychology of the comic vision, we saw that the comic vision tends toward:

1. Complex conceptual schemes
2. A high tolerance for disorder
3. Seeking out the unfamiliar
4. A high tolerance for ambiguity
5. Divergent thinking
6. Critical thinking
7. Emotional disengagement from problems
8. Willingness to change one's mind
9. Pragmatism
10. A second chance
11. An embracing of physical existence
12. Nonseriousness.

In its social psychology, as we saw, the comic vision tends toward:

13. Antiheroism
14. Pacifism
15. Forgiveness
16. Equality
17. More sexual equality
18. Questioning of authority and tradition
19. Situation ethics rather than rules
20. Social integration.

Anti-Tragic and Anti-Comic Features

In religions we can find not only pro-tragic and pro-comic features, but anti-tragic and anti-comic features. We have not constructed lists of these features, but we might note that there is at least one anti-tragic feature and one anti-comic feature found in most religions.

The anti-tragic feature is that similar to all social institutions, religions do not encourage the focus on the individual that the tragic vision does. To survive as social institutions, religions simply could not encourage their members to be loners in the way many tragic heroes are. And they almost all criticize individual desires and attachments. The most basic religious injunction is to forget about oneself and one's own needs in order to serve God or other people.

The anti-comic feature widespread in religions is their essential seriousness. Most religions have a powerful presumption for seriousness, and against anything nonserious like humor, comedy, or even play. In all major religions, a serious attitude is considered better than a nonserious one. We may find this presumption misguided, but we need to acknowledge it.

In many religions the value placed on seriousness arises from the value placed on the sacred. By definition, the sacred is something we should be serious about. If Paul Tillich is right that religion is based on ultimate concern, then it is based on what we take most seriously. Any religion based on the sacred, then, will automatically encourage reverence toward that which is sacred. And to the extent that the sacred interacts with the rest of human experience, seriousness toward the sacred tends to spill over into the rest of life. Humor and playfulness generally are then discouraged as irreverent or at least irresponsible. As Ecclesiastes puts it, it is the fool who laughs, while the wise person scarcely smiles (7:4).

This predisposition toward seriousness is heightened in monotheistic religions by their understanding of God as a being incapable of humor. If humor is enjoying some incongruity in one's experience—some surprise—then an omniscient being could not experience humor because such a being could not be surprised. And even if God could be surprised, as Creator of the universe God could not enjoy the frustration of divine expectations, for any such frustration would indicate a defect in that creation. While we humans might laugh at the drunkard or the adulterer in a comedy, God could not enjoy the incongruity here.

In the Bible Yahweh does laugh, but the laughter expresses derision rather than comic delight. In Psalm 2, for example, "the kings of the earth stand ready, and the rulers conspire together against the Lord and his anointed king." But "The Lord who sits enthroned in heaven laughs them to scorn; then he rebukes them in anger, he threatens them in his wrath." As Reinhold Niebuhr points out, "There is no suggestion of a provisional geniality in this divine laughter.

Derisiveness is pure judgment."[2] Similarly, the laughter of the prophets is only the laugh of scorn, not the laugh of humor. In 1 Kings 18:25–40, for example, Elijah taunts the priests of Baal, ridiculing their god as powerless compared with Yahweh. After laughing at them, he has them slaughtered. The aggressiveness of laughter in the Bible can also be seen in the response of the prophet Elisha when he was taunted by a group of children for his baldness: "He turned round and looked at them and he cursed them in the name of the Lord; and two she-bears came out of a wood and mauled forty-two of them" (2 Kings 2:23–24). The Bible is so serious, we might say, that in it even laughter is taken seriously.

What can we say in response to this religious presumption for seriousness? Supposing that we accept the tenets of one or more of the major religions: is it always better to be serious than nonserious? Is seriousness even better most of the time?

We can grant that an important function of any religion is to tell us what is important in life. But that does not rule out nonseriousness. Indeed, telling us what to take seriously is implicitly telling us what *not* to take seriously. Buddha, Jesus, and many other religious figures told us not to take material possessions, wealth, and power seriously, for instance. What is the Sermon on the Mount but a presentation of things we should take seriously along with things we should *not* take seriously, such as "what you shall eat, what you shall drink, what you shall put on." While Jesus does not joke about excessive concern for such things, his spirit in passages like "Look at the birds of the air" and "Consider the lilies of the field" shows the comic attitude of not sweating the small stuff.

Most religions warn us not only against concern with our bodies, but against taking ourselves too seriously. One of Jesus' main criticisms of the Scribes and the Pharisees was that they thought too much, and too highly, about their own status and virtue. Buddhism goes further in encouraging us to not take ourselves seriously, with its doctrine of *anātman*— which states there is no enduring personal ego or self!

Some religions even encourage us not to take religious rituals, leaders, and texts too seriously. Jesus scandalized many because he attached little importance to purity laws and rules for the Sabbath and temple worship. Buddhism, as we'll see, with its emphasis on nonattachment, encourages us not to take rituals, rules, or even the Buddha too seriously.

The presumption for seriousness in religions is misguided when applied beyond the sacred to all of human life. Peter Berger, writing in the monotheistic tradition, put it well: "Only God is ultimately to be taken seriously. Everything human remains less than serious by comparison."[3]

Not only is there room for nonseriousness in religion, but it can serve as a healthy antidote to absolutism. Religions have a natural tendency to encourage blind obedience and zealotry, and to discourage careful thought about their practices and doctrines. This zealotry suppresses self-examination or self-criticism, even when the evil of what is being done should be obvious. In the 1980s, for example, tens of thousands of zealous Sunni and Shi'i Muslims slaughtered each other in the Iran-Iraq War, even though Islam clearly forbids killing fellow Muslims. The Crusaders' massacres of Jews, Muslims, and Eastern Christians, and the killing of Christians by other Christians in the religious wars of later centuries should be enough to remind us that unqualified seriousness can lead to great evil. Keeping a sense of humor, especially about oneself, blocks such fanaticism. As Conrad Hyers has pointed out, military and missionary zeal seem inversely proportional to comic awareness.[4]

Even when it does not lead to fanaticism seriousness can block mental flexibility and creative thinking. As Walter Kerr said, "Seriousness as such is not necessarily a more elevated attitude than the comic stance: seriousness as such may be the state of mind of a drudge."[5]

Religions, then, can accommodate comic as well as tragic elements. We turn now to explore these in world religions.

Chapter 6

Eastern Religions

*I*n exploring the tragic and comic elements in religions, it is useful to consider separately the religions that originated in India and China from Western monotheistic religions. The Western ideas of a single Creator, sin as an offense against God, linear time, and a Last Judgment followed by heaven and hell are quite different from Eastern ideas. As we shall see, the metaphysical and theological differences between East and West make a difference in their tragic and comic features.

Hinduism and Buddhism

In the first chapter we noted how religions generally share with tragedy and comedy a concern with life's problems. Hinduism and Buddhism are especially good examples. As one Hindu thinker put it, from ancient times the central concern in Indian thought has been "an overmastering sense of the evil of physical existence, combined with a search for release from pain and sorrow."[1] The question of how to deal with suffering motivates all of Buddhism. Siddhartha Gautama became the Buddha, the Enlightened One, when he discovered the nature of suffering and how to eliminate it. And because in Buddhism and Hinduism we are reborn thousands of times, our suffering is greater than in Western religions, where our earthly life ends in a matter of decades.

49

From the earliest parts of the Bible, Western religions have looked for the cause of suffering in human wrongdoing, in sin. In Hinduism and Buddhism, however, the problem of suffering is a matter not of sin but of ignorance or faulty perspective. The cause of suffering is not what we did wrong but what we thought wrong. And so the solution to suffering is not practical—to get God to stop punishing us, or to find a cure for diseases—but philosophical—to change our way of looking at the world.

The Hindu and Buddhist goal is not deliverance or salvation, but enlightenment—*moksha* in Hinduism, *nirvana* in Buddhism. In both religions enlightenment is described as similar to waking from a dream to see reality. Though they have different descriptions of this reality, the goal in both is to discover it rather than to change it or escape it.

How do we achieve enlightenment, and what is the reality experienced? We achieve it, according to both Hinduism and Buddhism, by becoming emotionally disengaged from the familiar world. We quiet the noise of ordinary consciousness and eliminate ordinary desires for such things as pleasure and power. Detachment and self-control are the cardinal virtues, as they are in the teachings of some Western mystics, such as Meister Eckhart.

What we experience in enlightenment is different in Hinduism and Buddhism. In Hinduism we experience the one, eternal, ultimate being—Brahman, which is identical with my real self; in Buddhism, where there is neither Brahman nor self, we experience blissful emptiness.

In both Hinduism and Buddhism, enlightenment is liberating. We come to see that what we have been treating as real, is not, and that true reality does not have the defects of the common sense world. Indeed, when we are enlightened, the problem of suffering evaporates.

The Anti-Tragic Features of Hinduism and Buddhism

Even from this cursory sketch of Hinduism and Buddhism, a contrast with the tragic vision begins to emerge. That vision celebrates the individual person struggling amid suffering. Struggle is deemed noble because the person's desire to escape suffering is seen as realistic and legitimate. In Hinduism and Buddhism, however, for different reasons, this celebration of the self and its desires is unacceptable. In Hinduism, *atman*, the self, is identical with Brahman, ultimate reality, but this self is not the ego, the ordinary subject of experience. Brahman, in fact, transcends personality and desire. In Buddhism there is no enduring personal ego to celebrate, neither human nor supernatural. In both religions, self-centered desire, like that of the tragic hero, is something to be overcome.

Buddhism teaches that desire is the source of suffering, so that an enlightened person eliminates suffering in eliminating desire. In Hinduism, too, suffering and desire are overcome together. According to the *Upanishads*, when we are enlightened, "a blind man is no longer blind, a wounded man is no longer wounded, and a suffering man no longer suffers."[2]

Not only would the vain desires of the tragic hero be evaluated negatively in Hinduism and Buddhism, but so would the hero's struggle against the misperceived source of the evil. Both religions see the enlightened person as having nothing external to combat, and so both would reject the Western heroic idea that life is a series of battles with outside forces. Alongside the virtues of detachment and self-control in both religions is *ahimsa*, or nonviolence, which contrasts sharply with the militarism of the tragic vision.

Hindus and Buddhists have other beliefs that are opposed to the tragic vision, the most central of which are the beliefs in karma and reincarnation. Karma is the natural justice built into the universe: good actions automatically lead to good consequences and bad actions to bad consequences. What we call suffering is the bad consequences of our previous actions. Some people who suffer appear to be innocent victims—newborn babies, for example—and some evildoers appear not to experience the bad consequences of their actions. But each person is reborn thousands of times, and karma works across lifetimes. If one's actions do not have consequences in that lifetime, they will in future lives.

To see how these beliefs clash with the tragic vision, we can pose the five questions in our Tragic Profile to Hinduism and Buddhism.

1. *Is suffering orderly and understandable?*

In the tragic vision, much suffering is undeserved and unexplainable, but in the system of reincarnation and karma, all suffering is deserved and therefore explainable. All of us are personally responsible for all the suffering in our lives. Suffering that is apparently innocent is in fact the result of our bad actions, perhaps in a previous lifetime.

2. *Is suffering avoidable?*

The tragic answer is No for most suffering. For the believer in reincarnation and karma, the answer is a qualified Yes. We can avoid doing bad actions and thus avoid their bad consequences. While we cannot avoid the consequences of our past bad actions, this unavoidability of karma is not viciously fatalistic, given our freedom to act better in our current life. Indeed, karma guarantees that our good actions now will bring us to a higher state in the future, eventually to an enlightened state in which there is no suffering.

3. *Does suffering always at least have the potential to bring about some greater good, or is some suffering pointless?*

In the tragic vision, *some*, and maybe *most* suffering is pointless. In Hinduism and Buddhism, karma, as cosmic natural justice, is supremely good, and suffering is integral to that justice.

4. *Will everything work out for the best in the end?*

The tragic answer is No. For the believer in reincarnation, it is Yes. After some number of reincarnations, each person will find *moksha* or *nirvana*. No soul is irreversibly lost.

5. *How should we react to suffering?*

In answering the first four questions, I have been treating suffering in the way the tragic vision does, as something objective. But in philosophical Hinduism and Buddhism, suffering is a function of our perspective and attitude. It arises from our desires, and can be controlled by controlling our desires. So the Hindu or Buddhist response to suffering is quite different from the tragic response. While the tragic hero sees suffering as unavoidable and shows noble resistance, the Hindu and Buddhist react to suffering by changing their perspective and attitude. The tragic vision puts the spotlight on the individual person and emphasizes his or her nobility in suffering. In Hinduism and Buddhism, we escape suffering by escaping the illusion of that individual self. The response they advocate is not to dig in our heels and resist suffering, nor to bemoan our fate, but to get free of the self-concern that causes suffering.

The Pro-Comic Features of Hinduism and Buddhism

As might be expected, these religions with their anti-tragic features have pro-comic features. Many of them, in fact, are the same features. The belief in reincarnation, which gives each soul countless chances to achieve enlightenment, for example, is pro-comic and anti-tragic. Nonviolence, which inclines Hinduism and Buddhism away from the tragic vision, inclines it toward the comic vision.

The most important of these double-entry features is emotional detachment. In both Hinduism and Buddhism, enlightenment involves experiencing the incongruities in life without suffering, and that is possible because emotional detachment blocks fear, anger, sadness, and other negative emotions. That same attitude, as we saw in earlier chapters, lies at the heart of humor. What Buddhists call nonattachment is often called "distance" in comic theory. Henri Bergson called it an "anesthesia of the heart."[3]

Besides these double-entry features, Hinduism and Buddhism have other pro-comic features. We examined a family of them in chapter 4 under the heading "mental flexibility." These include complex conceptual schemes, a high tolerance for ambiguity, and divergent thinking. Hinduism and Buddhism hold that reality is very different from what appears to us. In Buddhism there are no substances: the apparently enduring personal egos we seem to experience are not real, and all is in constant change. Hinduism teaches that the whole world of ordinary perception is *maya*, appearances that can mislead us about the ultimate nature of reality. In reality there is only one thing—eternal, changeless Brahman. Looking at the world as these religions ask us to calls for huge shifts in our perspective, and to the extent that we continue to live in the familiar world, calls for great mental flexibility.

Not surprisingly, mental flexibility is valued in both Hinduism and Buddhism. Each religion takes many different forms, with different rituals and different explanations for the same things. Understanding even a few forms of one of these religions requires conceptual agility. Hinduism alone has some 330 million gods and Hindus are free to believe in all of them, some of them, or none of them. They may think of gods as persons, features of the universe, fictions, and so forth. Shiva—the oldest god in the world—is both male and female. Male gods have female consorts, who can be thought of as part of the deity. Because gods appear in many forms under different names, what seems to be a different deity can be just another form of one deity. Even Hindu monotheists tend to see Hindu polytheists as just worshipping different forms of their one god.

In India this mental flexibility and tolerance extends to what Westerners would call non-Hindu religions. Hindus sometimes take their children to mosque on Fridays to be blessed. Followers of Vishnu consider Gautama Buddha to be an avatar, an incarnation, of their god.

A colleague of mine once got into a discussion about Jesus with a young man from India. When the man said that he accepted Jesus as divine, my colleague asked, "Then you are Christian?" "No, I'm Hindu," the man replied. He accepted Jesus as divine, but also Buddha, Shiva, and many others.

The tolerance for ambiguity, the ability to switch perspectives, and the other forms of mental flexibility we have been discussing are characteristic of the comic vision, as we saw in chapter 4. The experience of amusement is enjoying a conceptual shift, as at the punchline of a joke. Amusement at jokes, in fact, is strikingly similar to Hindu and Buddhist descriptions of enlightenment. In both experiences, something new suddenly strikes us. We make sense of what has gone before in a new way. We "get it," and that brings delight. As an example of this "Aha–Haha" connection, consider this passage from Philip Kapleau's *The Three Pillars of Zen*:

> Afternoon dokusan [interview with the roshi, the master]! . . . Hawklike, the roshi scrutinized me as I entered the room, walked toward him, prostrated myself, and sat before him. . . . "The universe is One," he began, each word tearing into my mind like a bullet. "The moon of Truth—" All at once the roshi, the room, every single thing disappeared in a dazzling stream of illumination and I felt myself bathed in a delicious, unspeakable delight. . . . For a fleeting eternity I was alone—I alone was. . . . Then the roshi swam into view. Our eyes met and flowed into each other, and we burst out laughing. . . . "I have it! I know! There is nothing, absolutely nothing, I am everything and everything is nothing!" I exclaimed more to myself than to the roshi, and got up and walked out.[4]

If this is the effect of enlightenment on a beginner, is it any wonder that the Buddha is usually portrayed as smiling?

Hinduism

So far we have been considering Hinduism and Buddhism together, but each has distinctive features relevant to the tragic and comic visions. Let us consider some of these in Hinduism.

One pro-comic feature of Hinduism is its celebration of biological life. As in the comic vision, bodily functions like eating and sex are considered healthy. Hindu temples swarm with life—plants, cows, monkeys—and representations of life. Ganesha, the popular god of good luck, has the head of an elephant. The celebration of animal life is sometimes expressed comically, as in the *Ramayana* epic, where Rama's sidekick is the monkey god Hanuman.

In a way that can make puritanical Westerners uncomfortable, sexuality is celebrated in Hinduism. The *Kama Sutra* is famous for its sexual detail. Some Hindu temples are adorned with sculptures of couples (and triples and quadruples) in dozens of sexual positions. The great god Shiva himself is venerated in the form of a *lingam*, phallus, set in a *yoni*, vagina.

It is true that philosophical Hinduism teaches that reality is mental rather than physical, and some Hindu scriptures recommend the renunciation of the physical, associating holiness with asceticism. That strain in Hinduism can be seen as anti-comic. But the far more widespread forms of Hinduism celebrate biological life in all its diversity and fecundity.

Even the idealistic strain in Hinduism is not without its comic side, for it emphasizes enlightenment, which, as we have seen, is similar to, even overlapping with, amusement. The idealistic teaching that ordinary experience misleads us about the nature of ultimate reality, seems to make the whole world into a gigantic practical joke. Our goal in seeking enlightenment is to "get it." That's the comic happy ending par excellence.

Many of Hinduism's pro-comic elements can be found in gods like Ganesha, the elephant-headed "Remover of Obstacles," and Krishna, who is venerated as playful child, trickster, and lover. Hinduism also has real-life comic role models like Mohandas Gandhi, whose wit was as famous as his pacifism and egalitarianism. When asked by a British interviewer, "What do you think of Western civilization?" Gandhi answered, "I think it would be a good idea." "If I had no sense of humor," he said at another time, "I should long ago have committed suicide." It was because of his egalitarian comic vision that Gandhi opposed such traditions as the caste system and sacrificing the widow on the husband's funeral pyre.

Buddhism

Buddhism is an especially interesting religion to study in relation to tragedy and comedy, because its First Noble Truth, that life is full of disappointment and suffering, is the starting point of tragedy and comedy. The other three Noble Truths show that Buddhism inclines toward the comic vision rather than the tragic vision. These truths are: the cause of suffering is desire, suffering can be overcome by overcoming desire, and desire can be overcome by following the Eightfold Path (right views, right intentions, right speech, right action, right liveli-hood, right effort, right mindfulness, and right concentration). For Buddhism, suffering is not something objective and inevitable, to be endured with tragic defiance. It is a subjec-tive coloring of the way we look at things, caused by our emo-tional attachments. The basic Buddhist message is similar to the message of comedy: Step back emotionally from the world, and things get better. Buddha said that to eliminate suffering, we must eliminate our attachment to things. Freud said that when we laugh about something, we spare ourselves the emotions we would have felt toward it, and we refuse to let it have power over us.[5]

In Buddhism the recommendation that we be nonat-tached is no mere bit of self-help advice, but is based on meta-physical reflection. Enlightenment is not just becoming nonattached, but realizing why nonattachment is the right attitude to have toward the world and toward ourselves. In ordinary experience, according to Buddhism, we are able to crave things and people, because we take them and ourselves to be stable. We think of things and persons as substances that stay the same through time. If I have my heart set on owning that mansion on the river by the time I retire, for example, I assume that at that future time, there will exist a building identical to the one I see today, and more importantly, there will be a man identical to the man I am today. I believe that the future mansion will be the one I am looking at, and that the future man will be me. Even if I desire to buy the mansion today, I assume that I can hold on to it because it and I will stay the same into the future. But all such beliefs underlying my desire are false. From moment to moment nothing stays the same, neither the things in my world nor the bundle of psychological events that I call my mind. Everything is in constant flux. There are no unchanging substances and so there is nothing permanent that I could call my "self." Craving anything not only is a source of discontent but is irra-tional. There are no enduring objects or subjects.

To reach nonattachment, Buddhism uses meditation exercises. The simpler ones free us from attachment to things such as food, and the more sophisticated ones free us from higher attachments such as the attachment to self. All of them have comic overtones. Consider the exercise that Buddhaghosa, a meditation master of the fifth century C.E., used to free his disciples of gluttonous desires. He had them think in detail about how they obtained their food, how it was digested, and how it was excreted. Since monks beg for food, he first asked them to meditate on how they had to leave the peace and quiet of the monastery and travel to the village to beg. "On your way to the village, you meet with many nasty sights and smells, walking on rough roads full of stumps and thorns. . . . When you walk in the village, your feet sink deep into the mud, or the wind covers you with dust, and flies land on you. Some people give you no food, others give you stale or rotten food, others are rude to you." Next Buddhaghosa had them think about how grotesque eating is. Crushed by the teeth and smeared with saliva, chewed food becomes repulsive slop, "like dog's vomit in a dog's trough." It passes to the stomach, "which resembles a cesspool that has not been washed for a long time," then on to the abdomen, where it becomes feces and urine. Badly digested food, the master continued, causes "hundreds of diseases, such as ringworm, itch, scab, leprosy, eczema, consumption, coughs, dysentery, and so forth.[6] We need not go through all ten stages of this meditation, but it seems clear that by the end, Buddhaghosa would have succeeded in killing anyone's appetite for quite some time. Also notice how this meditation uses two standard comic techniques—the piling up of details, and exaggeration. Indeed, it sounds very similar to a speech by Falstaff or a stand-up comedy routine.

The best known Buddhist meditation exercises come from Zen Buddhism, a tradition rich in humor. Consider this Zen poem by Masahide:

> My house burned down.
> Now it's easier
> To see the rising moon.

More sophisticated than Zen's liberation from attachment to food and shelter is its liberation from attachment to words, concepts, and logical thinking. We are attached, according to Zen, when we treat logical thinking as a form of power and control, when through our words and concepts we try to "capture" or "master" the world. But understanding through concepts is inferior in at least three ways. First, it is a mediated kind of knowledge, while Zen seeks direct experience of reality. Secondly, concepts mislead us because they are static, while reality is in constant flux. And thirdly, conceptual thinking works by making distinctions, especially between opposites—mind/matter, subject/object, good/bad—while reality is essentially a unity. Our minds cannot be prevented from forming concepts and through them attempting to freeze, divide, and control the world—that is just the way the mind works. But we need to remind ourselves that any conceptual system, however useful in a particular situation, is at best a tool and not a direct contact with reality. We must constantly challenge our conceptual systems, according to Zen, and "break up" our concepts, to prevent ourselves from thinking that they give us an objective grasp of things.

This nonattachment to concepts and conceptual systems is related to the even more important nonattachment we mentioned earlier—from the mind itself thought of as a substance. The most basic attachment we must break is to the "I," the empirical self, treated as an enduring subject distinct from the rest of reality. In being liberated from that mistaken attachment to the self, we overcome the core of the problem of all attachment.

In helping us break attachments to things, words, concepts, and self, humor is valuable for its fostering of critical thinking and mental flexibility. It gets us out of mental ruts and blocks negative emotions, allowing us to face what might otherwise be disconcerting truths, such as that there is no self. What better way to treat such a realization than as a kind of cosmic joke my mind has unwittingly played on itself?

Almost any sudden realization may trigger laughter. Enlightenment and amusement often overlap, as we said earlier. In his book *Three Pillars of Zen*, Philip Kapleau cites a report of enlightenment by a Japanese business man who had just come home from meditation exercises at a Zen monastery. Drifting off to sleep, he was thinking about a line from a Zen classic.

> At midnight I suddenly awakened. At first my mind was foggy, then suddenly that quotation flashed into my consciousness: "I came to realize clearly that Mind is no other than the mountains, rivers, and the great wide earth, the sun and the moon and the stars." And I repeated it. Then all at once I was struck as though by lightning, and simultaneously, like surging waves, a tremendous light welled up in me, a veritable hurricane of delight, as I laughed loudly and wildly: "Ha, ha, ha, ha, ha, ha! There's no reasoning here, no reasoning at all! Ha, ha, ha!" The empty sky split in two, then opened its enormous mouth and began to laugh uproariously: "Ha, ha, ha!"[7]

Zen is especially famous for its use of humor to break up our attachment to logical thinking. As long as our thinking is going smoothly, we tend not to question the nature of thought and of ourselves, just as when our car is running smoothly, we tend not to look under the hood. But humor throws a monkey wrench into our thinking, and thus prompts us to question it. Koans like "What did your face look like before your parents were born?" and "What is the sound of one hand clapping?" force us out of our mental ruts, much as stand-up comics often do. Here Steven Wright comes to mind with comments like "My neighbor has a circular driveway—he can't get out!"

Exchanges between Zen students and masters often involve illogical shifts of thought, as when Tozan was asked, "What is the Buddha?" and answered, "Three pounds of flax." And answers to students' questions need not have any meaning at all. Rinzai, who founded one of the two great schools of Zen, would often reply, no matter what the question, with "Kwatz!"—a meaningless sound. Indeed, a question may be "answered" without words: the master may slap students or twist their noses. The purpose of all this nonsense and slapstick is to derail the rational mind, so that students can break their attachment to it.

There is one last kind of nonattachment that we should mention, which is also fostered through a shocking kind of humor. Zen masters teach that our attitude toward Buddhism itself can be a form of attachment, if Buddhism is thought of as a creed to which we subscribe or a set of rituals we follow. So there are no rituals, scriptures, doctrines, or religious figures—not even the Buddha—to whom we should become attached. Even the idea of nonattachment is not something to get attached to!

To break these attachments, Zen uses iconoclastic humor. Sengai (1750–1837) has a drawing of a meditating frog with a grin on its face. The inscription: "If by sitting in meditation, one becomes a Buddha"; the implicit punch line: "then all frogs are Buddhas." Another drawing by the same master shows a small boy leaning over to fart: its title is "The One Hundred Days Teaching of the Dharma." The master Tanka (738–824), according to a famous story, stopped for lodging at a temple where the deep snow prevented the monks from getting firewood. Tanka took one of the three wooden images of the Buddha from the altar and used it for firewood. When a monk asked the master Ummon (862–949), "What is the Buddha?" he answered, "A wiping stick of dried dung!" Before him Tokusan (780–865) had said, "The Buddha is a dried piece of barbarian dung, and sainthood is only an empty name." There is even a Zen saying, "If you meet the Buddha, kill him."[8]

It may seem a big jump from the teachings of the Buddha to this iconoclastic humor, but if the goal is nonattachment to everything, then the Buddha would not want his followers to show excessive reverence even for him. The comic spirit here may have brought a smile even to, or especially to, the Buddha's face.

Since all these irreverent stories about Zen masters are repeated for emulation, moreover, Zen clearly has comic role models. Even the Buddha's own story, with his prince-to-pauper reversal and his discovery of nonattachment as the secret of life, can be read as comic.

While both Hinduism and Buddhism have several anti-tragic and pro-comic features, then, Buddhism, especially Zen, seems more comic than Hinduism. Both religions hold that the world of common sense is misleading, and both therefore have a sense of irony about everyday experience. But in Hinduism behind the appearances is an ultimate reality—the one, eternal, unchanging Brahman. In Buddhism there is no such absolute. Nothing lies behind the common sense world, all is in constant flux, and the world is empty. That metaphysics, I suggest, is more comic than the metaphysics of Hinduism. Socially, too, Buddhism seems more comic because it is more egalitarian. There are no elites or castes; all people have the same essential nature, all are potential Buddhas.

Chinese Religions

When we move from the religions born in India to those of China, we encounter some major differences. While metaphysical, theological, and epistemological questions often arose in Indian thought—about the soul and self, life after death, the gods, time, reality and illusion—the Chinese showed little interest in such questions. They were more interested in practical issues like how to cure illness or govern a village or empire. In Chinese religions even the gods are mostly ancestors who can help them or harm them.

This practicality makes a difference when we look for tragic and comic features in Chinese religions. While Hinduism and Buddhism announce their concern with the nature of human suffering and its elimination, for instance, Confucianism and Taoism do not.

In Chinese thought, too, the universe is a harmonious unity in which each part reproduces the whole. The human body is a microcosm of the universe—we know that our blood circulates, for example, because we know that rivers flow. The Chinese acknowledge that life has it moments of need and pain, but those are just part of the harmonious whole, rather than something to be questioned, or, as in tragedy, something to be protested.

Because of this practicality, Chinese religions are metaphysically and epistemologically simpler than Indian religions. While those religions taught that the real world is not what most people think, Chinese religions generally accept the world of common sense as the real world. There is no metaphysical surprise awaiting us, as in Hinduism and Buddhism, and so living with a sense of irony—that great source of both tragedy and comedy—is not common in Chinese religions. Concern with the next life, so influential in Hinduism and Buddhism, is also missing.

Chinese religions do share with Hinduism and Buddhism certain anti-tragic features, though they are grounded differently in Chinese thought. Like the religions from India, Chinese religions lack the focus on the individual struggling amid suffering. They do not celebrate the individual at all—not for the Indian metaphysical reasons, but because their vision of human life is thoroughly social. Nor do they celebrate struggle, again not for Indian reasons, but because they do not see life as a series of conflicts. One of the oldest Chinese ideas is that things and their properties divide into *yin* and *yang*—female and male, dark and light, mysterious and clear, wet and dry, and so forth. These are opposites, but in Chinese thinking opposites complement rather than battle with each other. As the *Tao Te Ching* (6) puts it, "Opposition is the source of all growth."⁹

Without the celebration of the individual struggling amid suffering, both Indian and Chinese religions lack the heroic vision of tragedy. But Chinese religions also have their own anti-tragic features. Most importantly, as we mentioned, they do not put the nature and elimination of suffering high on their agenda. This is not to say that they are not concerned with floods, crop failures, and disease. Many of their religious ceremonies are conducted to block or get rid of just such evils. But in Chinese religions, dealing with suffering means getting food for the village during a famine, not pondering a philosophical question about the nature of suffering. Like all cultures, the Chinese face mistakes, sickness, hunger, and death; but that does not prompt them to ask whether Heaven owes them something better. Without a philosophy of suffering, tragedy just does not get started in Chinese religions.

Chinese practicality is not just anti-tragic but pro-comic, as is their emphasis on the social group over the individual. Another pro-comic/anti-tragic feature, not found in the religions of India, is their emphasis on body rather than spirit. The Chinese do not see the real human being as something immaterial. Whether or not there are spirits, we are not spirits, and our concerns are those of embodied people. For this reason, celibacy and asceticism did not take hold in Chinese religions.

Thus, we can say that Chinese religions lack important features of the tragic vision and have some features of the comic vision. But how comic are they? Could we call either of the great Chinese traditions, Confucianism or Taoism, a comic vision of life? Here we need to look at these traditions individually.

Confucianism

No single person has had more influence on Chinese culture than Confucius. Temples were built to him in all two thousand counties of China, and well into the twentieth century he was honored as divine.

Confucius was born in the middle of the sixth century B.C.E., when feudal warfare in China had caused serious cultural decline. His vision was to return his society to greatness by reinvigorating the rituals, virtues, and social institutions of what he saw as the Golden Age, represented best by the rule of the Duke of Chou in the twelfth century B.C.E.

In the ideal state described by Confucius in the *Analects*, rulers would lead not by force, or even by laws, but by moral example. Their main virtue, which would be everyone's virtue, was *jen*, "humaneness." The other virtues Confucius mentioned most were filial piety, loyalty to rulers, good faith, and ritual propriety.

Later generations of Confucian scholars emphasized the importance of filial piety and loyalty, interpreting them not merely as respect for, but as blind obedience to parents, ancestors, and rulers. Such virtues, of course, were just what many emperors wanted from the people, and so they made Confucian teaching a foundation of education for civil service, and education in general. A few centuries after Confucius, *The Book of Filial Piety* was written. It was so effective in fostering obedience that in the tenth century someone forged a similar work singing the praises of sub-servience to the ruler. Called *The Book of Loyalty*, it was passed off as an ancient Confucian classic. In the *Analects*, loyalty had meant doing one's best in the service of a ruler, not blind obedience. Mencius, the second greatest figure in Confucianism, had opposed unquestioning obedience to rulers. But no matter, the Confucianism promulgated by the royal courts was used to bolster public support for their reign, and it fostered conservatism in politics and in thinking gener-ally.

Are there tragic or comic aspects to Confucianism? We said earlier that Chinese thinking generally tends away from the tragic vision because it lacks a focus on the individual struggling amid suffering. And this is certainly true of Confucianism. Does Confucianism have comic tendencies? It certainly has the three pro-comic features mentioned earlier as characteristic of Chinese thought—practicality, an empha-sis on the social group, and an emphasis on the body over the spirit. Confucianism also has several other pro-comic fea-tures.

First, Confucianism is relatively egalitarian. Like other traditional religions, it is sexist, but it is not elitist in ranking certain classes as better than others. Confucius did not reject the traditional four Chinese classes—scholars, farmers, arti-sans, and merchants—but did teach that such distinctions were irrelevant. As in the comic vision, everybody counts. Morally, too, there is no upper class. Everyone from peasant to emperor can achieve goodness. Mencius said that everyone may become a Yao or Shun (legendary wise emperors).[10]

The egalitarianism here shows in the Confucian attitude toward education, which in China has always been the devel-opment of character as well as the acquisition of information and skills. Confucius wanted to make education available to all males. Indeed, in the *Analects* (15. 38), it says that if there is education, there are no class distinctions.

This emphasis on education shows another pro-comic feature in Confucianism—its basic confidence in human beings. Mencius said that human nature is essentially good, so we can hope to inculcate *jen* in everyone. Confucius thought that *jen* was rare, but still achievable by everyone. What was needed were leaders who themselves manifested *jen*, to lead the people by moral persuasion.

Because Confucianism believes in everyone's educability and potential for goodness, it emphasizes moral persuasion, rather than threats and force, as the way to motivate people. It shows an opposition to militarism, which is also a pro-comic trait. This is evident especially in Mencius, who taught that violence has no lasting benefits—the only good way to rule, he said, is by virtuous example.

Beyond its optimism about human beings, Confucianism is optimistic about life as a whole. The impersonal force called Heaven, which deals out life and death for us all, is provident: things work out in the long run.

Despite all these pro-comic features, however, Confucianism stops far short of a comic vision of life, primarily because of its mental rigidity. It emphasizes order, discipline, obedience, loyalty, ritual propriety, historical precedents, and similar patriarchal values, and so it lacks the freedom and playfulness of the comic spirit. If the gentleman is not grave, the *Analects* say, he will not inspire awe in others.[11] In each situation there is one proper way to act, and so there is little room for comic imagination or even for seeing things from different points of view.

The comic spirit is critical of institutions and power, and so governments have always been wary of comedy. But Confucianism supports order, tradition, and the status quo, and so it has been popular with all kinds of governments for thousands of years. It has encouraged not critical thinking but conformity.

Confucianism, despite its highly social philosophy, is not a comic vision of life. A more promising candidate for the comic vision is the other Chinese indigenous religion, Taoism.

Taoism

The word Taoism is applied to many things—a philosophy of life, religious rituals, alchemy, and divination. We will concentrate on the Taoist philosophy of life, looking for aspects relevant to the tragic and comic visions of life.

The Tao is ultimate reality, but unlike God and Brahman, is neither spiritual nor above the everyday world. Unlike God, the Tao is not a person, has no desires, and does not interfere in events. There is no exact English equivalent for "the Tao," but "Nature" comes close, if we mean by it not the things in the universe, but, as the dictionary says, "the power, force, principle, and so forth that seems to regulate" them.

Like Confucianism, Taoism lacks the tragic focus on the individual struggling amid suffering, and does not have a tragic vision of life. But while Confucianism also lacks a significant tendency toward the comic vision, Taoism has a number of important pro-comic features. We can find these, along with several anti-tragic features, in the *Tao Te Ching* of Lao Tzu, the main text of Taoism. The theme of this work is that we should accept what is natural, and pattern our lives after Nature. The Tao moves through our lives and we should let it move as it will. There is no room for resistance, rebellion, or even manipulation. In more detail, Taoism teaches:

1. Nature underlies everything. All events occur in Nature.
2. Things and qualities in Nature appear as opposites (*yin/yang*) that work together. "Opposition is the source of all growth" (6).[12]
3. Nature does not exert itself. Nature includes everything, and so all events are internal to Nature. There is nothing for Nature to act *on*. "Nature never acts, yet it activates everything" (37).
4. What happens in accordance with Nature is good. "The truth is that whatever is natural is good" (50).
5. Human beings are part of Nature and so find their happiness living in accordance with Nature. Indeed, "Whoever acts naturally is Nature itself acting" (23).

In this vision of life, the tragic outlook can scarcely get a foothold. As in Confucianism, the concern with undeserved, unexplainable suffering is missing. Taoism admits the existence of evil, but tends to attribute it to human beings. "Nature is already as good as it can be" (29). "Nature's way is to produce good without evil" (81). When we suffer, it is because we are somehow working against Nature; if we would just go along with the natural order of things, we would be happy. While anyone with tragic sensibilities can easily imagine a world better than this one, Taoism holds that Nature "cannot be improved upon. He who tries to redesign it, spoils it" (29). Also, because Nature offers us the best possible world here and now, this life is sufficient. There is no inclination to look to a next world for happiness or for the meaning of life, as is common in Western religions.

Moving Taoism further away from the tragic vision, and closer to the comic vision, is its egalitarianism. As we have seen in our tragic-comic contrasts, the tragic vision is based on social elitism, the comic vision on equality. The *Tao Te Ching* opposes hierarchical systems, not only in society, but in our thinking in general. All things are equally natural, and so humans are no more important than other things, nor are some humans more important than others. Nature itself evens out extremes: "Nature's way is to take away from those that have too much and give to those that have too little" (77). That kind of reversal is itself an important theme in comedy.

Another pro-comic, anti-tragic tendency in Taoism is its opposition to heroism and militarism. We will be happiest, Taoism teaches, when the opposite forces in our lives work together rather than conflict, and when we let things happen rather than trying to cause them to happen. This view optimistically minimizes action, especially the use of force. Militarism is the epitome of forceful action, and so is rejected, along with its heroic ideology. The *Tao Te Ching* condemns war as a way to accomplish anything, for "Force will be met with force, and whenever force is used, fighting and devastation follow" (30). "The one who follows Nature avoids weapons, for they create fear in others" (31), and "the more weapons people possess, the more they fight" (57). The *Tao Te Ching* has a line that sounds like something from Danny Kaye's comedy *The Court Jester*: "Just as a fish should not be taken out of water, so a sword should not be taken from its scabbard" (36).

Taoism does not categorically exclude all fighting, but when a wise person is forced to use weapons, "he does so with reluctance and restraint" (31). "The best soldier does not attack. The superior fighter succeeds without violence. The greatest conqueror wins without a struggle" (68). Again, these ideas are found in many comedies.

In rejecting hierarchy, militarism, and heroism, Taoism rejects the values they place on pride and honor. "The inner self is our true self; so in order to realize our true self, we must be willing to live without being dependent upon the opinions of others. . . . Pride attaches undue importance to the superiority of one's status in the eyes of others. . . . When one sets his heart on being highly esteemed, and achieves such rating, then he is automatically involved in the fear of losing his status" (13).

Along with the rejection of hierarchy and force goes a distrust of authority and government, and a celebration of rural simplicity. "When government governs little, people are happy. When government governs much, people are miserable" (58). "The more laws are enacted and taxes assessed, the greater the number of law-breakers and tax-evaders" (57). "The ideal state is a small intimate community" (80), an agrarian society in harmony with nature.

As we would expect, the virtues advocated by Taoism are not heroic virtues like ambition and courage but pro-comic virtues like gentleness, frugality, and humility, the "Three Jewels" of Taoism. The leading virtue is *wu-wei*, active nonstriving, effortlessness. *Wu-wei* is very similar to the ancient comic ideas that we accomplish most by what we do not do, or by what we do without trying, themes found in comedy ranging from the play *Lysistrata* to the characters of Falstaff and Tom Sawyer.

Chuang Tzu, the second most important figure in Taoism, writes with comic irony that "Nonaction makes a person the lord of all fame; nonaction serves him as the treasury of all plans; nonaction fits him for the burden of all offices; nonaction makes him the lord of all wisdom. The range of his action is inexhaustible, but there is nowhere any trace of his presence."[13]

As a role model for the comic vision, Chuang Tzu goes beyond Lao Tzu. While the *Tao Te Ching* was addressed to rulers, Chuang Tzu is opposed to government. His writing is often wildly fanciful, and he parodies other more straitlaced ideologies. Unfortunately, his playfulness was often missed by his readers, and the imaginative sections of his writing have often been taken literally by religious Taoists. The passages about flying "supermen" who, dining on air and sipping dew, were immune to heat and cold and lived forever, were interpreted as descriptions of "The Immortals" by Taoists who then tried to figure out how to secure their own immortality. But Chuang Tzu himself would have laughed at both their misinterpretations and their attempts to use magic to live forever. Death is utterly natural, he taught, and not something to be avoided or feared.

Indeed, in Taoism all of our lives are to be accepted rather than manipulated. The *Tao Te Ching* says:

> There is no greater misfortune than desiring to change oneself—being discontented with one's lot.
> There is no greater vice than desiring to change things. . . .
> Only he who is satisfied with whatever satisfactions his own nature provides for him is truly satisfied. (46)

Acceptance of life also means accepting other people. "There is no greater evil than desiring to change others" (46). Intelligent people "let each thing develop in its own way, without any attempt to intervene" (64) and "without trying to impose [their] own ideas upon the lives of others" (63). They accept each person's way as best for that person. That, of course, involves the comic virtues of tolerance and acceptance.

Besides all these pro-comic features, Taoism also advocates freedom, spontaneity and the mental flexibility we have spoken of so often in connection with the comic spirit. "Wise behavior adapts itself appropriately to the particular circumstances" (8). This flexibility includes being weak rather than strong at appropriate moments. "The tougher fighters are more likely to be killed, and the harder trees are more likely to be cut down," Lao Tzu said. "At birth a man is soft and weak—yet capable of living the whole life ahead of him. At death, he is hard and tough—yet unable to live for even a minute longer" (76). Nothing is softer than water; and nothing harder than rock; yet flowing water wears down the hardest rock (78).

Conclusion

Eastern religions have several pro-comic features, and the visions of life in two Eastern traditions—Taoism and Zen Buddhism—can be said to be comic. On the other hand, Eastern religions, although sometimes concerned with suffering, have not developed a tragic vision of life, largely because they have not had the heroic concern with the individual struggling amid suffering. To find a tragic vision in religion, we need to turn to Western monotheism.

Chapter 7

Western Religions

Monotheism

At the beginning of the last chapter we noted that the differences between Western and Eastern religions make a difference in their tragic and comic features. The essential idea in Western monotheism, on which everything else depends, is the idea of one personal God. God structures all of human life and experience. Life is good or bad, fulfilled or unfulfilled, happy or miserable, as a function of our relation to God. If life is tragic or comic, or some combination of the two, it is in relation to God.

God is central in the Western tradition because He made everything and has a plan for everything. He has specific expectations for each kind of creature, especially for human beings, the pinnacle of His creation for which He made the rest. Because God requires obedience to His will, he promulgated it—hence the divine law in the scriptures of Judaism, Christianity, and Islam. He is constantly evaluating humans for their compliance with His plan. Sometimes He is so angered at their failure to do what he wants that He kills large numbers of them. With the Flood He killed everybody except for one family.

Our basic relationship to God is that we live either in fulfillment of His plan or in violation of it. In Judaism, we keep or fail to keep the covenant. In Christianity, we do or fail to do the will of God. In Islam we submit or fail to submit to God—

the very term "Islam" means "submission." All three ideas come down to obedience and disobedience.

These three religions hold that humans have often disobeyed God, and so He has punished them throughout history. Eventually, as most adherents of the three faiths hold, God will conduct a Last Judgment of the whole race and start a new order, one that will last forever. A standard belief is that all those who have died will be brought back to life for judgment, and for the reward and punishment that will follow it. In some Jewish and a few Christian belief systems, there will be a new order on earth. In most Christian and Muslim sects, the afterlife will consist of two states: heaven, a state of perfect happiness; and hell, a state of total misery.

Connected with the Last Judgment is the Messiah. In Christianity, God has already sent a Messiah—Jesus Christ—to usher in a new age and to rescue the human race from its sinfulness, and he will reappear at the time of the Last Judgment. In Judaism and Islam, the Messiah has not come yet; he will appear when the human race has followed God's will and created a good world.

So in most forms of monotheism, what hangs on our fulfillment or nonfulfillment of the divine plan, our obedience or disobedience to God's will, is our happiness in this life, our eternal happiness in the next life, or both. The idea of eternal happiness or misery, of course, has enormous implications for whether life is tragic or comic. In most tragedy and comedy life is measured in decades and there is no absolute happiness or misery. If life is in fact unending, and if the second, eternal stage of life is either perfectly happy or perfectly miserable, that changes everything.

We will be considering the three monotheistic religions individually, but before we get into details, let us look at the tragic and comic aspects shared by Judaism, Christianity, and Islam.

The Pro-Tragic Features of Monotheism

If we were asked whether Judaism, Christianity, and Islam are more similar to tragedy or to comedy, it would be reasonable to say tragedy. These traditions are fundamentally serious, even solemn, in their mythology, in their rituals, and in their historical, metaphysical, and ethical teachings. The revealed scriptures in all three traditions are serious documents, written in ancient languages and in dignified, often heroic styles. Almost all of the commentaries on these scriptures, as well as the other writings in these traditions, are uniformly serious.

Serious is not equivalent to tragic, but with tragedy the three monotheistic religions also share the belief that life is full of suffering. And there are characters in the scriptures who react to suffering with a tragic spirit, such as Job and Ecclesiastes in the Hebrew Bible, and Jesus on the cross crying out, "My God, my God, why have you forsaken me?"

Added to the seriousness and sense of suffering in the monotheistic scriptures is a fatalism mirroring that in the tragic vision. In this tradition, God knows the whole future. Indeed, before we are born, God knows what we will do and experience at each moment—including, in Christianity and Islam, whether we will be saved or damned. According to the Bible, God has even manipulated certain people's minds to make them act in certain ways. In Exodus 9:12, for example, He hardens Pharoah's heart so that he will not listen to reason and let the Jews leave Egypt. John's Gospel has a fatalistic explanation for the rejection of Jesus:

> In spite of the many signs which Jesus had performed in their presence they would not believe in him, for the prophet Isaiah's utterance had to be fulfilled: "Lord, who has believed what we reported, and to whom has the Lord's power been revealed?" So it was that they could not believe, for there is another saying of Isaiah's: "He has blinded their eyes and dulled their minds, lest they should see with their eyes, and perceive with their minds, and turn to me to heal them." (John 12:37–40)

In the Gospels, Jesus knows people's future actions. On the night before the crucifixion, Jesus told his apostles that one of them would betray him. He tells Peter that before morning Peter will have denied him three times. These are not wise predictions based on good evidence, but knowledge of the future. The sense that the future has been predetermined by

God, like a book or script already written, is strongest, perhaps, in Islam, where kismet was declared an item of Muslim
faith in the middle ages.

The Anti-Tragic Features of Monotheism

Counterbalancing their pro-tragic features, the monotheistic
religions have several anti-tragic features. First, unlike classical tragedy, which is humanistic, monotheism is God-cen-
tered. The monotheistic religions discourage the self-concern
of tragedy.

In classical tragedy the characters are noble in part
because they pursue *their own* purposes, and live by *their own*
wills. By contrast, in monotheism, humans are supposed to
subordinate their desires to the will of God. Our purpose in
living is not something we invent, but the purpose God has
for us. Our purpose can be ours only in the sense that we
accept it, that we align our wills with God's will. That is why
in all three religions morality is obeying God.

Just as tragic heroes are up to their own purposes, they
suffer on their own. Their nobility arises in part from their
forlornness. However, in monotheism, when we are carrying
out the will of God, we are never on our own. All suffering,
indeed all of life, should be experienced in relation to God. In
moments of suffering, we can ask God for relief. He may provide it, but even if the suffering does not end, we can trust
that what we are experiencing is for the best in His divine
plan.

The sting of tragedy is that someone's suffering does not
serve a higher purpose, but is unredeemed, pointless. In
monotheism, on the other hand, God is provident: He controls all events for our good. In the big picture, nothing is out
of place or wasted. Even when human beings rebel against
God, their actions fit in with His master plan. *Whatever* happens, including all instances of evil, is the will of God, and is
ultimately for the best. Even the innocent suffering of children is not pointless. As humans with limited knowledge we
may not understand how this or that suffering is for the best.
But we believe that it is, and that no one is mistreated by God.

Since God's providence is allied with His omniscience and omnipotence, too, no one has good reason to question or protest any event. No one could know better than God, or have a better master plan than His, and so it is irrational to rebel against God's will. In monotheism, the proper response to apparently tragic events is humility, patience, resignation, and forbearance. Failing to submit to God's will is not just irrational; moreover it is the essence of sin. All of this runs counter to the spirit of the tragic hero, whose central feature is a strong-willed resistance toward fate, even a divinely ordained fate.

Another feature of monotheism that is opposed to tragedy also arises from its "divine-will ethics." In tragedy, moral dilemmas are common, and Antigone's feeling of being in the wrong *whatever* she does is an important tragic feeling. But in monotheism, what is right is what God wills, and God never wills contradictions. So we are never in a situation where we are in the wrong whatever we do. There are no true moral dilemmas.

The Pro-Comic Features of Monotheism

Although the monotheistic religions are fundamentally solemn, they do have non-solemn moments, such as institutionalized celebrations and moments of spontaneous joy. Celebration and joy are not by themselves comic, but they figure in many comedies. Another pro-comic feature of monotheistic religions is their lack of concern with worldly success, power, wealth, and glory. Again, similar to comedy, these religions are opposed to ambition.

This opposition to ambition is related to two more pro-comic features of monotheistic religions, their egalitarianism and their favoring of the poor and the less fortunate. Like comedy, these faiths root for the underdog.

More importantly, all three faiths console us in moments of suffering that things are not as bad as they might appear, because God is still in charge of the universe, and in the long run things will work out. This religious detachment from our daily troubles is similar to the emotional distance of comedy.

The Anti-Comic Features of Monotheism

Counterbalancing these pro-comic elements in monotheism are a greater number of anti-comic elements. One is that at each moment, the universe and each of our lives is moving either in the right direction or in the wrong direction. Each moment is judged against God's standards, and we are always capable of falling. In traditions like Calvinism, we are depraved and capable by ourselves of nothing but falling. There is an urgency to each moment, then, as the prophets, Jesus, St. Paul, and Muhammad reminded us. With a constant orientation to God's will and to the Last Judgment, there is no "time out," no room for play, no leisure time. As Jesus said, for every idle word we will be held accountable on the day of judgment (Matt. 12:36).

Because the Bible and the Qur'an hold as their primary value the following of God's will, they are to that extent incapable of advocating the enjoyment of what goes against God's will, such as human vice and stupidity, which make up the bulk of what is laughed at in comedy. At the heart of the comic vision is an ability to enjoy the incongruity in our experience, including our own incompetence, failure, and moral shortcomings. But enjoying such incongruity is incompatible with monotheism, because when things are not as they should be, that is a matter for concern, not delight!

To understand this tension between comedy and monotheism, the most direct approach is to ask if God Himself has a sense of humor. The God of the Bible and the Qur'an is our ultimate role model, and while He shares many characteristics with humans, a sense of humor is not among them. He is a warrior, a father, a king, and so forth, but never a trickster, a clown, or even someone who is amused. There are a few biblical references to God's laughter, but they are to the laughter of scorn, not to the laughter of amusement. If we understand the Bible as God's revelation about Himself, then we can say that God has no sense of humor.

But if God cannot be amused, then to what extent could He approve of our doing so? Consider the standard laugh-getters in comedy from the days of Aristophanes—laziness, greed, lechery, gluttony, pomposity, and self-deception. These are all vices that call forth God's judgment. Could there be any room in His plan for our laughing at them rather than morally judging them, as He does?

If God is thought to be too exalted a role model, then consider the human role models in the scriptures—Abraham, Moses, St. Paul, Muhammad—none of whom is presented as praiseworthy for having a sense of humor. The only one of this group even described by the scriptures as laughing is Abraham. But his laughter, when he is told that his elderly wife will bear a child,[1] is based on his ignorance and his lack of trust in God. It is not something we are supposed to emulate.

With this general understanding of Western monotheism, we can now turn to the three religions in the tradition.

The Tragic Vision in the Hebrew Bible

The monotheistic tradition begins with the Hebrew Bible, and for Judaism, Christianity, and Islam, its ideas are foundational. So it is a good place to begin our search for tragic and comic elements in Western religions.

Of all the scriptures in the monotheistic religions, the Hebrew Bible is the longest and the most varied. Composed and edited by dozens of people over centuries, it contains creation stories, law codes, folk wisdom, military history, love songs, genealogies, prophetic warnings, apocalyptic visions, and more. It presents no single unified philosophy of life. Some of the writings are optimistic, some pessimistic. Some portray God as intimately involved with the world, others do not even mention Him. So it would be wrongheaded to ask if the Hebrew Bible as a whole is tragic or comic. What we can do is look for tragic and comic features in its various books, and for overall tendencies and patterns emerging in them.

We can begin by looking for pro-tragic features. An obvious one is militarism. Like Greek tragedy, much of the Hebrew Bible was created in a warrior culture with a heroic tradition that celebrated strength and conquest. Many of its books are written in elevated, heroic language. God Himself is sometimes described as a warrior and the Israelite army as "the hosts of Yahweh." Militarism and heroism are not sufficient for a tragic vision of life, of course, but they show a tendency toward that vision.

The Hebrew Bible also contains many themes and stories found in tragedies. God's asking Abraham to sacrifice his son Isaac, for example, sounds like tragedy, and Kierkegaard saw in Abraham a strong similarity to the tragic hero. The major theme of all tragedy, the fall from happiness to misery, is found throughout the Hebrew Bible, starting with chapter 3 of Genesis. Almost the first thing that Adam and Eve do is disobey God. For that they are expelled from Eden and condemned to toil, suffer, and die. From then on, humans disobey God over and over, and he punishes them over and over. As in Greek tragedy, guilt and punishment are collective and inherited as well as individual. God punishes whole tribes and cities—even the whole human race in the Flood—and he punishes the descendants of evildoers.

Although there are hundreds of characters and events in the Hebrew Bible, the overall story is the history of a group, the people of Israel. While they experience great triumphs and moments of celebration, their story as a whole reads much like a tragedy. At the end of the Bible, they are living unhappily under foreign occupation. Not long after that, Jerusalem would be destroyed and they would be scattered.

God chose Israel to be a great nation, a beacon to the world. He worked miracles to get them out of bondage in Egypt. Then He created a covenant with them through Moses, and gave them laws to live by and a land to live in. But they break the covenant, worship false gods, and call down God's wrath. God forgives them each time, and even sends prophets to keep them on the right track, but they disobey again and again. God uses the Assyrian armies to wipe out the ten northern tribes, and then the Babylonians to take the two southern tribes into captivity. When the Persians invade Babylonia, some of the Israelites return home with new hope. They rebuild the temple in Jerusalem. But their dreams are not fulfilled as they live under Persian domination. In another two centuries the Greeks conquer them, and for a time they are persecuted. Then come the Romans. In 70 C.E. a Jewish rebellion against the Romans is crushed, the temple is destroyed, and the people of Israel are scattered. For the next two millennia, there would be no nation of Israel.

What makes this story sound tragic is not only its general decline but its air of inevitability. In Greek tragedy, events set in the future were as determinate as events in the past. Most people did not know what those events were but oracles and seers like Teiresias in *Oedipus Rex* did. The people of Israel, with their omnipotent and provident God, also thought of the future as determinate. Corresponding to the Greek oracles are God's prophets. Not only does God know the future so that it has to happen the way He foresees, but He often directly causes events. He even causes mental states in people to get the results He wants. When Moses was pleading with Pharoah to let his people out of Egypt, for example, not only did God say that Pharoah would not agree, but He "hardened Pharoah's heart" so that he would not agree (Exod. 9:12). Similarly, the Bible says that God used the Assyrian and Babylonian armies to punish the Israelites: presumably, it would not have been possible for the Assyrians or Babylonians to refrain from attacking the Israelites.

As in classical tragedy, the story of the Israelites also gets more troubling as it goes on. In the early days of the covenant of Sinai, they won many battles, took land and spoils, and prospered. The world seemed understandable and fair: when we follow God, He will bless us; when we disobey Him, He will punish us. But then they found that the world was not such a tidy merit system. Defeat and suffering seemed more random. Not all bad deeds were punished, and some good deeds were followed by suffering. At the end of the Hebrew Bible, Jews are suffering torture and death precisely for their faith in God. Such undeserved and unexplainable suffering is at the heart of the tragic vision.

One indication of the Israelites' growing decline was the emergence of prophetic visions of future greatness. In prosperous times, people celebrate their present; in times of decline, they look to a past or future Golden Age. When the Northern Kingdom of Israel fell to the Assyrians in the eighth century,

Isaiah prophesied that the Assyrians would be crushed and Israel restored. When the southern tribes of Israel were captive in Babylon, Second Isaiah envisioned God anointing and arming the Persian emperor Cyrus to liberate them. He also envisioned a restoration of the nation of Israel and a conversion of the whole world to Israel's God. In the last three centuries B.C.E., when the Jews were often oppressed under foreign domination, apocalyptic and messianic visions abounded. The vision of Daniel, written during a persecution of the Jews in the second century B.C.E., is especially revealing, for it adds to the great day of liberation a resurrection of some of the dead: "Many of those who sleep in the dust of the earth shall awake; some shall live forever, others shall be an everlasting horror and disgrace" (Dan. 12:2–30). Isaiah had foreseen a day when God would vindicate the Israelites by resurrecting them while leaving their enemies dead. "Dead they are, they have no life, shades that cannot rise; for you have punished and destroyed them. . . . But your dead shall live, their corpses shall rise; awake and sing, you who lie in the dust" (Isa. 26:14, 19).

These are the only two visions in the Hebrew Bible of the dead coming back to life, and they are visions of miraculous events, not teachings about human beings in general. The understanding of death throughout the Hebrew Bible is that it is the end of personal existence—there is no heaven or hell to compensate for this life. God himself never mentioned anything beyond death—His words in Genesis were clear: "Dust you are, to dust you shall return" (3:19). But because these prophetic visions promise something unusual, they indicate how miserable conditions probably were at the times they were written.

So far, we have been looking for tragic features in the story of the people of Israel, but in the last few centuries B.C.E. Biblical writers extended their tragic reflections beyond the fate of Israel to the human condition itself. Here they focused on two facts about life: innocent people sometimes suffer greatly, and each person's life comes to an end after a few decades. The two books that present these reflections most systematically are Job and Ecclesiastes. We can consider them one at a time.

Job

The idea that suffering is punishment for sin was so entrenched in the early Bible that when apparently innocent people suffered, questions were raised. When God tells Abraham that He is considering destroying Sodom, for example, Abraham asks if He really would destroy an entire city for the sins of only some of its inhabitants (Gen. 18:16–33). "Far be it from you to do this—to kill good and bad together; for then the good would suffer with the bad. Far be it from you. Shall not the judge of all the earth do what is just?" In the story, it turns out that the whole city was utterly evil and so deserved to be destroyed (except for Lot's family, who are allowed to escape). But the point is clear: God should not inflict suffering on the innocent. As the Hebrew Bible progresses, however, there are cases in which God appears to do just that. But how could He?

That is Job's question. Job is a paradigm of innocent suffering; indeed, he is singled out to suffer just because he is so righteous. God proudly asks Satan, "Did you notice my servant Job? There is no one on earth like him; a man of perfect integrity, who fears God and avoids evil" (1:8).[2] Satan answers that Job's faithfulness has been easy, given his prosperity, health, and loving family. "But just reach out and strike everything he has," Satan says, "and I bet he'll curse you to your face." God accepts the challenge and allows Satan to first take away Job's wealth, then kill his children, and last, afflict him with a hideous disease.

Job does not curse God as Satan had bet, but in his intense suffering, he does curse his own birth, and he demands to know why God would allow him to suffer so. Three of Job's friends rehearse the traditional theodicy that suffering is punishment for sin; so, they say, Job must have done something wrong. But Job insists that he has not.

Once Job begins to think about the unfairness of his own suffering, he generalizes to the human condition.

Man who is born of woman—
    how few and harsh are his days!
Like a flower he blooms and withers;
    like a shadow he fades in the dark.
He falls apart like a wine-skin,
    like a garment chewed by moths.
And must *you* take notice of him?
    Must *you* call *him* to account?
Since all his days are determined
    and the sum of his years is set—
look away; leave him alone;
    grant him peace, for one moment.
Even if it is cut down,
    a tree can return to life.
. . . .
But man is cut down forever;
    he dies, and where is he then?
              (14:1-10)

Job is finally disgusted by the inflexible arguments of his friends, and he makes his case before God. He has been God's faithful servant, he argues, and has lived a highly moral life. If he deserves punishment for anything, let God tell him what it is. "Isn't disgrace for sinners and misery for the wicked?" (31:3)

    Job's description of his plight sounds like classic tragedy:

Terror rises before me;
    my courage is blown like the wind;
    like a cloud my hope is gone.
And now I am in agony;
    the days of sorrow have caught me.
Pain pierces my skin;
    suffering gnaws my bones.
Despair grips me by the neck,
    shakes me by the collar of my coat.
You show me that I am clay
    and make certain that I am dust.
I cry out, and you do not answer;
    I am silent, and you do not care.

You look down on me with hatred
   and lash me with all your might.
You toss me around in storm clouds,
   straddle me on the wind.
And I know that you will destroy me
   and lock me in the house of the dead.

(30:15-23)

God responds to Job's complaint in a voice from a storm, not by recounting any wrong Job has done, nor by explaining his own wager with Satan, but with a rhetorical display of His power (chaps. 38–41).

Who is this whose ignorant words
   smear my design with darkness?
Stand up now like a man;
   I will question you: please, instruct me.
Where were you when I planned the earth?
   Tell me, if you are so wise.
Do you know who took its dimensions,
   measuring its length with a cord?
What were its pillars built on?
. . . .
Have you ever commanded morning
   or guided dawn to its place—
. . . .
Have you seen where the snow is stored
   or visited the storehouse of hail,
which I keep for the day of terror,
   the final hours of the world?
. . . .
Do you give the horse his strength?
   Do you clothe his neck with terror?
. . . .
Is your arm like the arm of God?
   Can your voice bellow like mine?

For four chapters God goes on, describing the mighty creatures and natural forces He has made. Finally Job is reduced to silence.

God's speech is powerful, but as a reply to Job it is a non sequitur. Job had not questioned God's power in creating the universe. He had asked a moral question—why would God inflict suffering on a faithful servant? The voice from the storm is quite outside the realm of morality. God presents no argument that He has treated Job justly. Indeed, at the end of the book He reprimands Job's friends for saying that He inflicts suffering only on those who deserve it: "You have not spoken as you ought about me, as my servant Job has done" (42:7). God even demands that they bring a sacrifice to Job and have Job intercede for them before him. Then, as if to admit that he has wronged Job, He doubles Job's previous fortune, and replaces his dead sons and daughters.

Stephen Mitchell has called the Book of Job "the great poem of moral outrage."[3] Job's family is killed, his land is destroyed, and he is afflicted with a horrible disease—for what? Because God wants to win a bet with Satan!

Had God explained the real reason for Job's suffering, Job's case would have been even stronger. But God does not. He does not even explain ordinary suffering. Instead, He changes the subject and stuns Job with an account of His power in nature.

The simple conclusion of the story is that God is not morally perfect. He does what He wants, sometimes helping people, other times harming them. The voice from the storm simply avoids moral questions. God does not even argue that might makes right. He says, in effect, "That's the way my universe works—it does not care about you."

If God's universe is an amoral arena of powerful forces clashing, as He implies, then it looks very close to the universe of the tragic vision. Much suffering is undeserved and unexplainable. We are not being rewarded or punished. We are simply struggling to get along in a dangerous world where no one is looking out for us. Because we are weak and ignorant, we do not do very well, and regardless of how well we do, in a few decades each of us is destroyed anyway.

Most commentators interpret Job's response to God at the end of the story as regret for having questioned God. If it is, then it is a nontragic response. But as God himself points out, Job's charges were accurate. Why, then, should he regret speaking the truth and asking for an explanation? Stephen Mitchell see Job's response at the end of the story as continued resistance, but in silence. Job covers his mouth, we could say, not because he has been given an explanation of how God is just, but because he sees that no such explanation is possible. He has been presented by God with a vision in which human beings with all their moral concepts and desires for justice simply do not count.

Ecclesiastes

If the book of Job extends the tragic vision beyond the fate of Israel to human suffering in general, Ecclesiastes extends it further by finding tragedy not just in suffering, but in life itself, even in the apparently successful life. The phrase often repeated is "emptiness, and chasing after the wind," which is applied to wealth, to success, to all striving.

The book identifies Ecclesiastes as a rich and successful king of Israel. "Whatever my eyes coveted, I denied them nothing" (2:10). Unlike Job, who had also been rich and successful, Ecclesiastes never experiences a reversal, but he still finds human life grossly unsatisfying. "In wisdom I applied my mind to study and explore all that is done under heaven. It is a sorry business that God has given men to busy themselves with. I have seen all the deeds that are done here under the sun; they are all emptiness and chasing the wind" (1:12-14). Wealth does not satisfy for long, nor does pleasure. Even his own wisdom is chasing the wind, for, while wisdom is preferable to folly, the same fate—death—overtakes both the wise and the foolish. Even moral distinctions do not matter in the face of death. "One and the same fate befalls every one, just and unjust alike, good and bad. . . . This is what is wrong in all that is done here under the sun" (9:2-3). And, to add post-mortem insult to injury, the fruits of all our labors are inherited by those who did not share our labor. "This too is emptiness and utterly wrong" (2:22).

Ecclesiastes emphasizes two tragic features built into life—death and chance. As in the rest of the Hebrew Bible, he understands death to be the end of the human person. So whatever we achieve comes to an end in a few years. Even the wealthy man leaves this life "naked as he came; all toil produces nothing which he can take away with him. This too is a singular evil" (5:15–16). Chance makes all our striving still more pointless, for the important events in our lives are not anything we choose. Sometimes good things happen, often bad things happen, but we are not in control. Even for the few decades of life we have, we do not know what will happen next. Whatever God's plan for the world might be, humans are not privy to it. "God has so ordered it that man should not be able to discover what is happening here under the sun. However hard a man may try, he will not find out" (8:17).

From our perspective, then—the only perspective we can live by—our lives are random and meaningless. "When things go well, be glad; but when things go ill, consider this: God has set the one alongside the other in such a way that no one can find out what is to happen next. In my empty existence I have seen it all, from a righteous man perishing in his righteousness to a wicked man growing old in his wickedness" (7:14–15). "Man is a creature of chance and the beasts are creatures of chance, and one mischance awaits them all: death comes to both alike" (3:19).

So not only is the life of great suffering, like Job's, tragic, but all human life is tragic. Of course, the Speaker notes, loneliness, injustice, and suffering only make life worse.

> I considered all the acts of oppression here under the sun;
> I saw the tears of the oppressed, and I saw that there was
> no one to comfort them. Strength was on the side of their
> oppressors, and there was no one to avenge them. I
> counted the dead happy because they were dead, happier
> than the living who are still in life. More fortunate than
> either I reckoned the man yet unborn, who had not wit-
> nessed the wicked deeds done here under the sun. (4:1–3)

How should we live, if life is cruel and futile? Here Ecclesiastes is quite pragmatic. We should "fear God and obey his commands" (12:13), for we live in his universe. But "Do not be over-righteous and do not be over-wise. Why make yourself a laughing-stock?" (7:16) Beyond that, the best we can do is to eat, drink, and enjoy ourselves for the brief span God has allotted us (5:18–19).

Although Ecclesiastes and Job are similar in many ways, Ecclesiastes does not challenge God as Job does. In the face of suffering and futility, he does not recommend the defiance of the tragic hero, or even the questioning of Job. Rather he advises us to fear and obey God. In that way he seems less tragic than Job. Surely, "Eat, drink, and be merry" is not a tragic response to life. But in his analysis of the human condition, Ecclesiastes is deeply tragic. He says that not only suffering, but life itself is random, unjust, and unintelligible. In that way, he goes beyond classical tragedy almost to a modern absurdist tragic vision.

There is more to the late Hebrew Bible than Job and Ecclesiastes, but these are the books that present a philosophy of life most carefully. If we put that philosophy together with the late Hebrew Bible's general pessimism about the fate of Israel, we have a generally tragic vision of both the people of Israel and human life in general.

The early Bible had not embodied a tragic view of life. The focus was on the people of Israel, and so as long as Israel was prospering or had hope of prospering, the death of the individual was not problematic. Life included suffering, but that suffering was understood as God's just punishment for sin.

As history went on, however, several things happened to make the Israelites' vision of life more tragic. First, the nation declined and there was more suffering. The northern part was destroyed. The southern part was taken into captivity, and even when released, they lived under a succession of foreign rulers. Second, much suffering began to look unfair, and that made the writers of the late Hebrew Bible question the understandability of suffering. Third, there was an increasing focus on the individual, especially on individual mortality. Even in a nation that lived forever and prospered, each person would come to a sorry end within a few years.

To see the extent of the tragic vision in the late Hebrew Bible, consider how it would answer the five questions in our Tragic Profile.

1. *Is suffering orderly and understandable?*

The late Hebrew Bible would answer No. We can discern no purpose to life in general and to human suffering in particular. There is no overall fairness in who suffers and how much.

2. *Is suffering avoidable?*

We can avoid only what we can foresee, and many big events in life—including calamities—we cannot foresee. God, on the other hand, foresees and controls all events. What He decides will happen, happens of necessity, and is therefore unavoidable.

3. *Does suffering always at least have the potential to bring about some greater good, or is some suffering pointless?*

Much suffering is pointless even in the short term. In the long term, death makes suffering, and everything in life, pointless.

4. *Will everything work out for the best in the end?*

Our individual lives are futile. If we consider the history of Israel, there is little evidence that it will flourish at some future time; and even if it does, it is not clear that the great suffering the people of Israel have gone through will have contributed to that prosperity.

5. *How should we react to suffering?*

There is no single answer in the late Hebrew Bible. Job might be our role model. If Stephen Mitchell's interpretation of the ending of the Job story is right, Job continues to resist, like a silent tragic hero. In that case, tragic resistance to suffering is what is recommended. If the traditional interpretation of the ending is right, then Job finally submits to God's power. But even then, God has admitted that Job's complaints were true, and has given no moral justification of His actions. So it remains reasonable to question all the unfair suffering in the world. Job's silence may simply be his admission that he is up against irrational power.

Ecclesiastes is a more practical and skeptical role model. He does not challenge God or even suggest that God might have set up the universe differently. What possible benefit could such a challenge produce? Like Job and Oedipus, he does suggest that the best fate of all is not to be born, but he does not curse his own fate or anyone else's. Like many modern thinkers, he simply advises us to make the best of a bad situation.

The Tragic Vision in Judaism after the Bible

In the last two millenia the people of Israel have moved to all parts of the globe, and have developed several systems of belief and practice. Early Judaism added the Mishnah to the Bible, a law code written around 200 C.E., and then the Talmud of Jerusalem (400 C.E.) and the Talmud of Babylonia (600 C.E.) commenting on the Mishnah. Later, in addition to mainstream Judaism came mystical movements like Kabbalism and Hasidism. In the last two centuries Reform Judaism, Conservative Judaism, and Reconstructionism have developed alongside Orthodox Judaism. Have all these developments over the centuries changed the essentially tragic vision found in the late Hebrew Bible?

Two beliefs have moderated the tragic vision somewhat. First, the idea of the Messiah, hinted at in the Bible, was developed. This figure will be a king sent by God to usher in a new age for Israel and for the whole world. He will not come like Jesus Christ to save us from our fallen state; rather he will come *after* we have created a good world and just society.

This belief looks to a better future, and so works against the tragic vision, but how confidently do Jews believe in the Messiah? For most Jews, is it a belief, or just a hope? In two thousand years the Messiah has not appeared, and treatment of Jews by Christians has been systematically bad over most of that time. What could be more in conflict with the prospect of the Messiah than the Holocaust? Some Jews even have joking expressions showing skepticism about the Messiah. "That will happen a week after the Messiah comes," for example, is equivalent to "That will happen when hell freezes over."

The second belief developed after the Bible that moderates the tragic vision, is belief in the resurrection of the dead. In the Babylonian captivity the Jews became familiar with Persian beliefs in a resurrection and a last judgment, followed by reward and punishment. These ideas involved a dualistic conception of the human soul as separable from the human body, however, something foreign to the Biblical understanding of the person, so they were not incorporated into the Hebrew Bible. But they did leave an impression on Jewish thinkers. When the Greeks conquered Palestine two centuries later, the Jews were exposed to the even less Jewish idea of a Platonic immortal soul. By late Biblical times, some Jews, notably the Pharisees, believed in some form of resurrection of the dead.

As the tradition of the Pharisees became rabbinical Judaism, ideas about resurrection and life after death spread and were developed. Some medieval rabbis, amalgamating current views, presented the following account. When the kingdom of Israel is reestablished in the future, righteous Israelites from the past will be resurrected to enjoy life in the new Israel. That state will not be permanent, however; eventually God will intervene to resurrect and judge everyone. After that, the righteous will be transported to a new world.

Like belief in the Messiah, beliefs in life after death offered hope, and that works against the tragic vision. If life is a two-stage process, then no matter how bad the first stage is, the second may make up for it, and so render life as a whole not tragic.

There has been no requirement that Jews believe in the Messiah or in life after death, but many have. By the twelfth century when Moses Maimonides compiled his list of thirteen principles of Jewish belief, these two beliefs were included.

Whatever Jews have believed about the Messiah or life after death, however, the emphasis in Judaism has always been on daily life here and now. Unfortunately, the reality of that life over the last two thousand years, especially in Christian Europe, was enough to keep alive the tragic vision, regardless of eschatological beliefs. Soon after the Christians gained political power in the Roman Empire, they began persecuting Jews, and that persecution has lasted into our own century. Not only could the Jews not reorganize a nation, but in most places the law prevented them from even owning land. Until the nineteenth century, most Jews saw themselves as living in exile. In the Crusades, Jews were slaughtered en masse. The Enlightenment improved the lot of some Jews, but then came the pogroms and the Holocaust, which for some called into question God's special relationship with the Jews, and even His presence in history. When the state of Israel was reestablished after two millennia, it brought new hope, but from its inception there were serious problems, between Jews and other groups, and between different groups of Jews.

After centuries of persecution and genocide, it is not unreasonable for Jews today, like those in late Biblical times, to accept the basic tenets of the tragic vision. Human beings do not understand their place in the world at all well. Life is full of suffering, much of it undeserved. Whatever God is, He is not simply beneficent. In Isa. 45:7 He said it Himself: "I form the light and create darkness; I make peace, and create evil: I the Lord do all these things."

If contemporary Judaism has role models, surely Elie Wiesel is among them. Wiesel tells of something he witnessed as a young man in one of Hitler's death camps. Three rabbis decided to put God on trial for what had happened to the Jews. They prepared their briefs, and over several days presented arguments against and for God. At the end they voted: the verdict was unanimous: "Guilty." The spirit of Job has survived well over the centuries.

The self-understanding of many Jews after the Holocaust also fits well with the tragic vision. If tragic figures are those who suffer greatly, reflect on their suffering, cannot understand it but yet are ennobled by it, then many Jews today see themselves as tragic figures. Indeed, they believe that their suffering makes for personal greatness and for the greatness of Judaism.

Pro-Comic Features in Jewish Culture

We have spent considerable time exploring the tragic vision in Judaism. Is there also a comic vision? Certainly Jewish popu-

lar culture is rich in humor. Scholars have written many
books on Jewish jokes, and Jews write and perform comedy in
far greater numbers than their proportion of the general popu-
lation would lead us to expect. But "Jews" and "Jewish" are
ethnic terms as well as religious terms. Is the tradition of Jews
in comedy traceable to a comic tradition in the religion
Judaism, or is it rather an ethnic phenomenon?

If there is a comic vision of life in Judaism, we should
expect to find it in the foundational writings of Judaism—the
Bible, the Mishnah, and the Talmuds of Jerusalem and
Babylonia. If there is no comic vision here, it is reasonable to
conclude that the religion Judaism does not have a comic
vision. We can begin by considering the Mishnah and the
Talmuds. Their central concern is to derive from the Bible
rules for governing all aspects of life—agriculture, eating, sex,
commerce, religious rituals, and so forth. The goal is to put
each thing, situation, and action into appropriate categories,
so that we may act as God has commanded. There are many
rules about purity and keeping things distinct, and several
hierarchical classification systems. Thousands of cases are
examined to determine exactly how to carry out the divine
commands in the Bible. These writings do present opposing
viewpoints, and in rabbinical schools students are encouraged
to analyze them and argue various interpretations of them. So
rabbinical training does promote logical and critical thinking.
Nonetheless, the whole enterprise of examining in detail
thousands of cases and rules makes all of life serious business,
and so is incompatible with the comic vision. The desire to
order and regulate everything shows such anti-comic features
as idealism, a low tolerance for ambiguity and disorder, and a
preference for the familiar. It is based on convergent rather
than divergent thinking.

If the Mishnah and the Talmuds do not have a comic
vision, what about the Bible? The strongest arguments for a
comic vision here come from scholars who have comic interpretations of Biblical stories. By examining their readings of
these stories, we can test the plausibility of the idea of a
comic vision in the Hebrew Bible.

Typical of these comic interpretations of Biblical stories are Conrad Hyers' reading of the book of Jonah as a satire on a reluctant prophet,[4] J. Cheryl Exum and J. William Whedbee's comic reading of the story of Isaac,[5] and Whedbee's reading of the book of Job as a comedy.[6] We can consider these interpretations one at a time, both to assess the arguments in them, and to ask what conclusions may be drawn if we accept these arguments.

The Book of Jonah is probably the strongest candidate for comedy in the Hebrew Bible, mostly for its generous use of two standard comic devices, exaggeration and fantasy.

Jonah hates the Ninevites and so at first refuses to accept from God the job of warning them. He wants them not to repent but to be wiped out by God's wrath. He is so reluctant, in fact, that he boards a ship to run away from God. God then creates a storm, and Jonah's shipmates throw him overboard to placate God, who next sends a huge fish to gulp down Jonah. Three days later the fish spits Jonah up on a beach, and he goes to Nineveh as commanded by God, to tell the Ninevites, "In forty days, Nineveh shall be overthrown." Uttering that one sentence causes everyone in the city to put on sackcloth and repent. God then spares Nineveh, but that so angers Jonah that he sulkingly asks God to end his life.

This summary is meant to emphasize the elements in the story that make it seem comic—its exaggeration and its fantasy. For the sake of argument, we can add the assumption that the author used these elements to make us laugh at Jonah for his foolish stubbornness. We can even follow Hyers in calling the story a satire, that is, a work in which vice, folly, and stupidity are held up for ridicule and contempt.

But granting all this, what follows? Could we conclude that the Book of Jonah embodies a comic vision of life? I do not think so. The strongest justifiable conclusion, I think, would be that the author of the Book of Jonah is trying to show the foolishness of resisting God's will. In attempting to escape from God, and in sulking after Nineveh is saved, Jonah is acting utterly unreasonably. To emphasize this folly, and so to teach us a moral lesson, the author uses exaggeration and fantasy. But even assuming that he intends for us to laugh at

Jonah, he does not encourage laughter more generally. He does not encourage laughter at all prophets, say, or at life's problems. The story's exaggeration and fantasy have a specific rhetorical purpose—to show the foolishness of opposing God's will—and are not evidence of the comic spirit toward life as a whole. While the story of Jonah may be a satire, it does not embody a comic vision of life.

With this lesson in mind, we can turn to our second Biblical story that has been read as comedy, the story of Isaac in Genesis. Exum and Whedbee claim that Isaac is "one of the *most comical* of Israel's ancestors,"[7] and they summarize their reasons in this way:

> First, its plot line, both in the parts and the whole follows the U-shaped pattern intrinsic to comedy [social integration followed by problems, followed by re-integration]. Though it indeed has its moments of near tragedy and pathos, each time we find the decisive upturn to a happy ending. Second, style and theme display comic traits: word plays are plentiful, especially the pivotal pun on Isaac's name; ludicrous and farcical moments abound; and comic irony and incongruity are pervasive. Finally, the characterization of Isaac as passive victim is best construed as comic.[8]

We can examine these reasons one at a time. What is problematic about the first reason, that the episodes in Isaac's life have a U-shaped plot, is that this plot structure is not unique to comedy, but is found in melodramatic plots, epic plots, and even some tragic plots.

Exum and Whedbee's second reason for claiming that Isaac's story is a comedy is that it has comic style and themes. The problem here is that classifying parts of Isaac's story as "ludicrous" and "farcical," and claiming that "comic irony and incongruity are pervasive," beg the question of whether Isaac should be read as comedy. While I would say that the story has irony and incongruity that *could be* presented in a comic way, I do not see that they were presented in a comic way in Genesis.

Irony and incongruity are not enough to make a story comic, for they are found in tragedy too, as well as epic, melodrama, and other literary forms. What is needed to make irony and incongruity comic is a playful attitude. In comedy, readers are led by the text to laugh at the characters and events. But I do not see that the irony and incongruity in the story of Isaac are presented this way. Exum and Whedbee say of Isaac "Again and again he is laughed over,"[9] but here they misrepresent the text. (I do not count Abraham and Sarah's laughter at the announcement that they will have a baby, as laughter at or over Isaac.) As Francis Landy points out, Isaac is *not* laughed at or over in the text, and the critical moments in his life, such as his asking his father about the sacrificial animal on the way to the mountain, are presented as grave rather than as funny.[10] Unless Exum and Whedbee can show a playful attitude toward the events in the story, they are simply not justified in talking about *comic* incongruity.

The "ludicrous and farcical moments" that Exum and Landy cite are similarly problematic. "The seemingly preposterous promise of a new baby, the eavesdropping Sarah who is discovered, the divine visitor who feels insulted, the tête-à-tête between Yhwh and Sarah who attempts to cover up her laughter by lying to her guest(s)—all these elements add up to something equivalent to Hebrew farce."[11] But do they? Are these moments in Genesis presented as something to laugh at? I do not see that they are.

As a third reason for claiming that Isaac is a comic character, Exum and Whedbee cite Isaac's passivity as a comic element. But the moments in which Isaac is a passive victim, such as his almost being sacrificed by his father, and his being tricked into blessing Jacob instead of Esau, are not described in a playful way that makes us laugh. Exum and Whedbee compare Isaac to Charlie Chaplin, but again Francis Landy has the right rejoinder: it is not when Chaplin is a passive victim that he is funny, but when he musters ingenuity and skill to confront the forces oppressing him.[12]

Let us turn to the last of the three Biblical stories we are considering, the book of Job. Whedbee cites several features of the Job story to show that it is a comedy. First, the story has considerable incongruity and irony. Second, it has a happy ending, as Job's fortune is restored and he is given a new family. And third, Whedbee says, the portrayals of Job, God, and the other characters involve caricature and parody. Again, we can consider these features one at a time.

The first features Whedbee cites, incongruity and irony, are not enough to make the story comic, as we have seen, for tragedy and other genres use irony and incongruity too.

The second feature, the happy ending, seems more typically comic, but happy endings are neither necessary nor sufficient for comedy. In one silent comedy, for instance, Buster Keaton's character is building a house. In the last scene the house collapses around him. In Keaton's film *Cops* the closing scene is a tombstone with Keaton's hat atop. The ending of *Dr. Strangelove*, as we mentioned in chapter 3, is an Air Force officer riding a nuclear bomb dropping from a B-52, starting World War III. Nor is the U-shaped plot sufficient for comedy. Most adventure stories and romances, many melodramas, and some historical works have a happy ending without being comedy.

Whedbee's appeal to the "happy ending" of the book of Job seems especially weak as evidence that the book is comic, given the incredible suffering Job has endured, and the unsatisfying way God has answered his questions. Indeed, God's overcompensation of Job at the end seems to imply an admission of divine guilt, hardly a "happy ending." Several critics have suggested that the current ending of the book was stuck on to the story late, in order to satisfy readers troubled by the apparent conclusion that God is amoral.

The third feature of the Job story that Whedbee offers for his comic reading is that the portrayals of the characters involve caricature and parody. The problem here is that to call some portrayal of a character "caricature" or "parody," it is not enough to know that the character shows a high degree of some trait, or even that the author has intentionally exaggerated some trait in a character. For exaggeration is not unique to comedy, but is found in melodrama and tragedy as well. A character's cruelty might be exaggerated in a melodrama, for example, without making that portrayal "caricature" or "parody." To classify a portrayal as "caricature" or "parody," we have to know that the author was *poking fun at* the character, was exaggerating the trait to make us laugh about the character. But Whedbee does not show that the author of Job was trying to get us to laugh at Job, God, or Job's friends. Indeed, it is difficult to imagine the reader who would react to the story of Job with laughter.

I find Whedbee's reading of Job as a comedy the weakest of the three readings we have considered and the comic reading of the story of Isaac the second weakest. The one argument I find plausible is that the author of the book of Jonah wanted us to laugh at this most reluctant prophet. But accepting that point, even accepting the book of Jonah as a satire, does not commit us to much. Assuming that the author of Jonah wanted us to laugh at Jonah, we cannot reasonably conclude that there is a comic vision of life in those two pages, much less in the whole of the Hebrew Bible. The prophet Elijah's ridicule of the priests of Baal in the First Book of Kings does not represent a comic vision in that book, as his then slaughtering them makes clear (18:25–40). Similarly, assuming that the author of the book of Jonah was ridiculing Jonah's rebellion against God, that ridicule does not seem to involve a comic vision of life.

The story of Isaac shows even less of a comic vision of life than the story of Jonah, and the vision of life in the book of Job, despite Whedbee's observations, seems thoroughly tragic.

If there were a comic vision in any of these books, we would expect to find comic role models in them, protagonists who have a comic spirit toward life. But it is hard to imagine three characters with less comic spirit than Jonah, Isaac, and Job. Nor are there other characters in these stories who are comic role models.

The Hebrew Bible as a whole, furthermore, seems to have no leading characters who are comic role models. Rather, the prophets—God's mouthpieces to the human race—are models of humorlessness. Recall the story of Elisha's cursing the children in the name of God for their laughing at his baldness, followed by God's sending the bears to maul the children (2 Kings 2:23). One leader in the Hebrew Bible who shows a sense of humor is Abraham: he laughs when God says that his aged wife will bear a child. But that laughter is not presented as something to emulate.

In the various writings of the Hebrew Bible, I conclude, there are a few instances of techniques that could have been intended to make readers laugh. But there is no encouragement of laughter toward the human condition generally, no comic vision of life. And, as we have seen, by the time of the late Hebrew Bible the Jewish vision of life is thoroughly tragic.

If the formative documents of Judaism lack a comic vision of life, as I suggested earlier, then it is reasonable to expect that the Judaism built on them also lacks a comic vision of life. I conclude that insofar as we can speak of a Jewish religious vision of life, it is mostly tragic. The rich comedic tradition in Jewish culture is best seen as an ethnic rather than a religious phenomenon.

The New Testament

Christianity grew out of Judaism, and shares with it most of the basic beliefs of the Hebrew Bible, which it came to call the Old Testament. But it also added the New Testament, and with it new beliefs, most importantly about Jesus and about life after death. These changes made a difference in the tragic and comic dimensions of the new religion.

The New Testament is considerably smaller than the Hebrew Bible, was written over a shorter length of time, and does not display the great diversity of views of the Hebrew Bible. There are minor differences between the Gospel writers' accounts of some events, and differences of emphasis, but on the whole, the New Testament shows a fairly unified worldview.

Like the Hebrew Bible, the New Testament teaches that God created the world and has a plan for human beings, who are on earth to carry out His will. Humans have often disobeyed God, however, and so have been punished. While some of Jesus' contemporaries taught that God's plan requires following the hundreds of detailed laws in the Bible, Jesus emphasized the spirit rather than the letter of the law, and for him that spirit was love. Love God with your whole heart, he taught, and love your neighbor as yourself.

Jesus' ethic of love made his teaching different from that of other Jewish teachers of his time. So did his teachings about the Last Judgment, and about heaven and hell. Everyone would be resurrected, not just some Jews, he said, and all would be judged by God. After the Last Judgment, some would be sent to eternal reward, others to eternal punishment. This teaching changed the understanding of life that dominated the Hebrew Bible. No longer a matter of six or seven decades, life was now understood to be infinitely long. Its first stage, before death, was infinitesimal both in duration and intensity of experience, compared to the second stage, which was infinitely long and perfectly happy for the saved, perfectly miserable for the damned.

We can now look into the tragic and comic ramifications of these changes.

Pro-Tragic/Anti-Comic Elements in the New Testament

Like the Hebrew Bible, the only Bible the first Christians had, the New Testament shows an overall gravity. Its central story is the life of Jesus, which has tragic-seeming elements. Christian "passion plays" have treated the story much like a classical tragedy. Jesus declared himself a king, but he was arrested, humiliated, and crucified like a common criminal. On the cross, he called out in apparent despair, "My God, My God, why have you forsaken me?" (Mark 15:34; Matt. 27:46). The Muslims find this story so unworthy of a prophet sent by God that they deny that Jesus was crucified.

The gravity of the New Testament can also be understood in light of political events in first-century Palestine. A millennium of Jewish history, half of that under foreign domination, had given the Jews a serious vision of life. In the second century B.C.E., after the revolt of the Maccabees, there had been a tenuous period of self-rule, but then the Romans took control of Palestine. A century later they would destroy Jerusalem, putting an end to the Israelite nation for the next two millennia. Jews at the time of Jesus had little evidence of anything to look forward to. What they saw was great suffering and no discernible overall pattern of justice.

Under Roman domination, many Jews hoped for a Messiah to bring them into a new age. Apocalyptic visions abounded and prophets such as John called on people to reform their lives. Like earlier prophets, they had a uniformly serious message of danger: the world as we know it is about to end. Much of Jesus' message was also in this vein of prophetic warning. We need to change our lives, he taught, to prepare for the judgment of God, and hanging on that judgment is either unending happiness or unending misery. For those who enter the "Kingdom of Heaven," life will be perfectly happy from then on, but for the damned, the rest of life will be worse than anything Job could even imagine. There could be no fate worse than hell.

The end of the world, Jesus warned, will be cataclysmic, "as it was in the days of Noah" (Matt. 24:37). At the Last Judgment, he implied, many will be damned. His advise to his followers was "Enter by the narrow gate. The gate is wide that leads to perdition, there is plenty of room on the road, and many go that way; but the gate that leads to life is small and the road is narrow, and those who find it are few" (Matt 7:13–14). Theologians have argued about the number of damned, but if even a tiny fraction of the human race—say a million people—spend eternity in hell, that has serious tragic overtones for humankind. A worldview in which a million of us suffer endless torture is significantly tragic.

Hell does not, moreover, merely cast a tragic pall over the end of life. Even for those who eventually go to heaven, keeping the prospect of hell before their minds throughout their lives would color the whole of life. As Jesus said, we have to be always on the alert. "Remember, if the householder had known what time the burglar was coming he would not have let his house be broken into. Hold yourselves ready, then, because the Son of Man will come at the time you least expect him" (Luke 12:39–40). In the twentieth century most Christian churches have not emphasized Jesus' teachings about hell, and some, like the Anglicans, have dropped hell as a doctrine, but Jesus in the Gospels, and the first nineteen centuries of Christianity certainly taught that eternal damnation was a real possibility for everyone, and that in hell "the devouring worm never dies and the fire is not quenched" (Mark 9:48).[13]

Jesus' teachings about the danger of hell incline his vision of life toward tragedy and away from comedy in another way, too, by squelching creativity. If everything we do, say, and think is judged by God's standards, and our eternal lives hang in the balance, then there is only one correct way to act, speak, or think in any situation—God's way—and every moment of our lives takes us either closer to heaven or closer to hell. There are no nonpractical moments in life and so, it would seem, no room for playfulness. As Jesus warned, for every idle word we will be held accountable at the Last Judgment (Matt. 12:36). Studies of creativity have shown that one significant obstacle to creative thinking in any activity is judging the outcome of that activity, especially by preestablished standards. If rewards and punishments are added to judgment, creativity is further reduced. In Jesus' teaching, where the judgment is divine and the reward and punishment are infinite, the squelching of creativity would seem to be at a maximum.

Anti-Tragic/Pro-Comic Elements in the New Testament

Despite Jesus's teaching about the Last Judgment and hell, and despite the overall gravity of the New Testament, however, there is much in the New Testament that inclines it away from the tragic vision and toward the comic vision.

The New Testament is built around Jesus, so if there is a comic vision in the New Testament, it should appear in Jesus. What do the Gospel writers say about him? Do they portray him as having a comic side?

None of the Evangelists describes Jesus as joking or even speaking playfully, but then we must remember that none of them says anything playfully himself. Maybe the Evangelists had poorly developed senses of humor and so overlooked whatever comic sensibility Jesus had. We should also remember that the Evangelists' purpose in writing was to make converts to the new religion. They may have consciously or unconsciously filtered out events in Jesus' life that might be thought incompatible with his urgent message or with his status as Messiah and Son of God.

Even with this possible filtering, and despite the lack of overtly comic material in the New Testament, however, the Gospels reveal several features in Jesus that are at once anti-tragic and pro-comic. For one, he opposed hierarchy and elitism. He had humble origins himself and always championed the poor and powerless. He would never qualify to be a tragic hero, but could qualify as a "little guy" or "underdog" in comedy.

Another pro-comic feature of Jesus was his quick-wittedness. The Gospels record his speech as full of clever sayings with at least the potential for humor. When he warned his followers about the incompatibility of wealth with holiness, for example, he said that it was easier for a camel to pass through the eye of a needle than for a rich man to enter the kingdom of heaven (Matt. 19:24). That startling image might well have gotten a laugh, at least from the poor people listening to him.

The Gospels describe several occasions when Jesus' verbal cleverness got him out of traps. When some Pharisees and followers of Herod asked him, "Are we or are we not permitted to pay taxes to the Roman Emperor?" for example, they thought he would say either to pay taxes, which would make him unpopular, or to not pay taxes, which would get him arrested. But Jesus cleverly asked them to show him the coin of tribute. When they handed him a denarius, he asked whose image and inscription were on it, and they answered "Caesar's." So he said "Pay Caesar what is due to Caesar, and pay God what is due to God" (Luke 20:20–26).

Similarly, when some Pharisees asked Jesus why his disciples had not followed rituals for washing before a meal, Jesus said that "nothing that goes from outside into a man can defile him. . . . It is what comes out of a man that defiles him. For from inside, out of a man's heart, come evil thoughts, acts of fornication, of theft, murder, adultery, ruthless greed, and malice; fraud, indecency, envy, slander, arrogance, and folly" (Mark 7:15–23). On another occasion when he was asked why he had not washed before eating, Jesus said, "You Pharisees! You clean the outside of cup and plate; but inside you there is nothing but greed and wickedness" (Luke 11:37–39).

In *The Humor of Christ*,[14] Elton Trueblood cites several of Jesus' sayings against the Pharisees as examples of humor, but I think that most of them are better read as expressions of exasperation or anger. Yet even if Jesus' sarcasm here was not intended as humor, at least we can say that it shows imagination and a sharp eye for ostentation and hypocrisy, which are pro-comic traits.

Another pro-comic feature of Jesus is his frequent use of reversals in his speech. Reversal worked for him much as it does in stand-up comedy today: it overturns standard ways of evaluating things and gets listeners to think in new ways. When the Pharisees challenged Jesus for allowing his disciples to pick grain to eat on the Sabbath, for example, he answered that "The Sabbath was made for the sake of man, and not man for the Sabbath" (Mark: 2:27).

The ultimate reversal was salvation, which Jesus described paradoxically: "Unless the grain of wheat falls into the ground and dies, it remains alone. But if it dies, it brings forth much fruit. He who loves his life, loses it; and he who hates his life in this world, keeps it unto life everlasting" (John 12: 20–36).

In many of Jesus' sayings, the reversal is of social ordering, as when he said, "Everyone who exalts himself shall be humbled, and he who humbles himself shall be exalted" (Luke 18:14), and "Many who are first will be last, and the last first" (Matt. 19:30). When Jesus' disciples tried to keep parents from bringing their children to him to be blessed, Jesus said, "Let the little ones come to me . . . for the kingdom of God belongs to such as these. I tell you that whoever does not accept the kingdom of God like a child will never enter it" (Luke 18:15–17).

His advice for people going to a banquet was to take the lowest place at the table—that way the host would ask the guest to move up to a higher place (Luke 14:7–11). Had there been stand-up comics in Jesus' day, they could easily have made a routine out of this idea.

Jesus showed thought-provoking reversals not only in his speech but in his actions. When at the Last Supper, his disciples were arguing about which of them was the greatest, Jesus told them that unlike earthly kings, who lord it over their followers, they must lead in humility. "The highest among you must bear himself like the youngest, the chief of you like a servant" (Luke 22:24–26). And to show them what he meant, he poured water into a basin and washed their feet (John 13:5).

The most striking reversal in speech and action recorded in the Gospels is probably Jesus' promise to the thief crucified next to him: "This day you shall be with me in Paradise" (Luke 23:43). In all the Gospels, that thief is the only person Jesus ever promised admission to heaven!

The mental flexibility in Jesus' reversals showed not just quick-wittedness, but also a personal openness to people, to what we today call diversity. He welcomed young and old, rich and poor, Jew and Gentile, sinner and saint, even a Roman army officer. His own apostles included fishermen and a tax collector working for the Romans. He was friends with several women, at least one a prostitute. Rather than dividing people into "Us" and "Them," he showed concern for everybody.

Jesus' freedom from sexism, tribalism, and moral provincialism shocked many. Some of the Scribes and Pharisees murmured, "This man receives sinners and eats with them" (Luke 15:1–2; Mark 2:15–17). Even though the injunction to welcome the stranger was repeated dozens of times in the Hebrew Bible, there was still considerable ethnocentrism. But Jesus tried to break down "Us versus Them" thinking. Many Jews despised Samaritans, for example, but he associated freely with them. Though Jews and Samaritans did not use vessels in common, Jesus asked the Samaritan woman at the well to draw him a cup of water (John 4:7–9). When he was asked "Who is my neighbor?" his example was the Samaritan helping the Jew who had been beaten by robbers (Luke 10:29–37).

Often Jesus expressed his ethic of love for all human beings in the image of a banquet. In one parable, he compared the kingdom of God to a great feast. The invited guests excused themselves at the last minute, and so the host told his servants to go out to the streets and alleys and highways to invite anyone and everyone. "I want my house to be full" (Luke 14:15–24).

Once while eating at the house of a leading Pharisee, Jesus advised his host not to invite family and friends to his parties, for they would invite him in return, and that would be his reward. Instead, he said, "when you give a party, ask the poor, the crippled, the lame, and the blind; and so find happiness. For they have no means of repaying you; but you will be repaid on the day when good men rise from the dead" (Luke 14:12–14).

Much of Jesus' ministry was centered around banquets. His first miracle was at a wedding feast: after the wine had run out, he made more from water, and as John tells it, (John 2:1–11) it was better than the wine the party had been drinking. When crowds got hungry after listening to him for hours, Jesus multiplied bread and fish for them to eat (Matt. 5:43–44; Matt. 15:32–38). Jesus' own Last Supper was a banquet, as is the Eucharist. When he was asked why his disciples did not fast, Jesus compared himself to a groom at a wedding: "Can you expect the bridegroom's friends to go mourning while the bridegroom is with them?" (Matt. 9:14–15).

Jesus was criticized for his "indiscriminate" socializing. Some Pharisees, according to Jesus' defense, called him "a glutton and a drunkard, a friend of tax collectors and sinners" (Luke 7:31–35; see Luke 5:33).

In his openness, Jesus understood and accepted people's foibles and shortcomings, another pro-comic trait. To lead his church he chose Peter, an impulsive fisherman who just before Jesus' arrest had said "I am ready to go with you to prison and death" (Luke 22:33), but then a few hours later deserted and denied him.

Jesus' tolerance for such weakness was tied to his spirit of forgiveness. He was always willing to give people another chance—not only his followers, but even those who crucified him. "Father, forgive them; for they do not know what they are doing" (Luke 23:34) could never be a tragic hero's last words.

This ethic of forgiveness put it above even worship in urgency. "If, when you are bringing your gift to the altar, you suddenly remember that your brother has a grievance against you, leave your gift where it is before the altar. First go and make your peace with your brother, and only then come back and offer your gift" (Matt. 5:23–24).

Jesus' spirit of forgiveness contrasted with the legalism of the Pharisees. Once when he was in the temple, they brought a woman to him who had been caught in adultery. Mosaic law required that she be stoned to death, they pointed out. "What do you say about it?" Jesus' response was simple: "Let him who is without sin throw the first stone" (John 8:1–11).

Not only should we forgive, he taught, but we should not even judge—that we should leave to God. Both judgment and forgiveness will come to us from God as we have judged and forgiven other people. "Pass no judgment, and you will not be judged; do not condemn, and you will not be condemned; acquit, and you will be acquitted; give, and gifts will be given you" (Luke 6:37–38). We get another chance, that is, to the extent that we give others another chance.

How many chances? When Peter asked Jesus, "Lord, how often am I to forgive my brother if he goes on wronging me? As many as seven times?" Jesus replied, "I do not say seven times: I say seventy times seven" (Matt. 18:21–22).

Another pro-comic trait that went along with this non-judgmental, forgiving spirit was love of enemies. "You have learned that they were told, 'Love your neighbor, hate your enemy.' But what I tell you is this: Love your enemies and pray for your persecutors" (Matt. 5:43–44). The idea of loving enemies shocked many listening to Jesus, as did his opposition to retaliation and even self-defense. Do not resist the evildoer, he said. "If someone hits you on the right cheek, turn the other cheek to him also. If someone wants to take your shirt away from you, let him have your coat too" (Matt.

5: 39–40). This pacifism was at odds with both Jewish and Roman morality.

For all of his tolerance, forgiveness, and nonviolence, Jesus nonetheless thought critically about social institutions and practices, another pro-comic trait. Sacrifice in the temple, for example, which began as a religious act, had become big business. The one time the Gospels record Jesus as getting angry was on entering the temple and seeing the money changers and dealers selling sacrificial animals. Overturning their tables, he said, "It is written, 'My house is a house of prayer,' but you have made it a den of thieves" (Luke 19:46).

As with rituals, so too with laws. For Jesus it was the motive and not the outward action that mattered, so laws as formulas for outward action were not important. In his mind all the laws came down to just two: Love God and Love your neighbor. Any other laws must serve these. Jesus had little patience for legalistic concern with the law for its own sake, and so he did not hesitate to cure the man with the withered hand on the Sabbath in the synagogue, or the woman who had been crippled by a spirit. When the president of the synagogue criticized him for healing the woman, Jesus said, "What hypocrites you are! . . . Is there a single one of you who does not loose his ox or his donkey from the manger and take it out to water on the Sabbath? And here is this woman, a daughter of Abraham, who has been kept prisoner by Satan for eighteen long years: was it wrong for her to be freed from her bonds on the Sabbath?" (Luke 13:10–17).

This anti-legalistic spirit and emphasis on love as the proper motive for all action, are a strongly pro-comic combination. In comedy, love trumps all other motives, and there is no concern with the letter of the law.

So far in tracing anti-tragic and pro-comic traits in Jesus, we have focused on his attitudes and his ethics. But besides these, he had important new teachings about life after death, which also inclined his worldview toward the comic vision. As Ecclesiastes showed, if all of our accomplishments and hopes come to an end at death, then it is easy to view life as tragic. But Jesus promised a happy ending to life for those who followed his way, the ultimate happy ending—perfect happiness forever.

In the tragic vision suffering is not redeemed nor is there compensation for it, but if there is heaven, then no matter how dreadful life on earth is, there will be compensation for it. In the Christian vision, any suffering in this life can now be treated as preparation for heaven. The bulk of our lives—the part infinite in both length and intensity of experience—is after death. Whatever we might suffer before death will pale into insignificance afterwards.

What made the idea of Heaven more comic than it might have been, among the Greeks, for example, is that eternal life was not thought of as the natural fate of human beings. Our natural fate in the New Testament, as in the Hebrew Bible, is extinction—returning to dust, as God said in Genesis. If we end up in heaven, it is not by any natural entitlement, but by the grace of God. Like most good things in comedy, it is a gift. Read in comic terms, the story of Jesus on the cross saying to the thief, "This day you shall be with me in Paradise" is the height of comic grace.

Jesus had many parables to explain the idea of grace, such as the story of the prodigal son (Luke 15:11–32), and the story of the laborers in the vineyard who all earned the same wage, though some worked all day, others for just an hour (Matt. 20:1–16). In Jesus' vision, as in comedy, life is not a system of merits and rewards. Many of the good things come simply by chance or by someone's generosity. Heaven is the ultimate example of such grace.

In tracing the comic aspects of the New Testament, we have concentrated on Jesus, but before leaving the topic, we might say a word about Saint Paul, the second most influential figure in the New Testament. Much of Paul's vision of life was pro-comic in ways similar to Jesus' vision of life. Most importantly, he was opposed to legalism and he subscribed to Jesus' ethic of love. Paul was also influenced by Greek thought, and so he added some pro-comic elements to Jesus' vision. First, he knew enough Greek philosophy to know the value placed on rational thought in the Greek world, and he realized that much in his new religion would not pass muster by philosophical standards. So, as followers of Jesus, he said, we must be prepared to look like fools for Christ's sake; he cheerfully embraced the image of a fool in the eyes of the world (I Cor. 4:10).

Working against this pro-comic element in Paul is the Greek, specifically the Platonic, denigration of the body in favor of the soul. While Jesus had held a Jewish monism in which the body is not something separate from the person, Paul had a more Greek view in which the body is the base part of us pulling us downward, and the soul is the good part of us striving upward. Our sexuality, which Paul saw as paradigmatically physical, was then paradigmatically base, and so to be avoided. He advised Christians to be celibate, or, if their sexual urges were just too strong for that, to get married as a last resort (I Cor. 7:9). This negative understanding of sexuality denigrated women, for they were the ones who elicited sexual desire from men. So while Jesus was not a dualist, did not denigrate the body or sexuality, and was considerably less sexist than his contemporaries—all pro-comic traits—Paul went in the opposite direction on all these issues.

Christianity after the New Testament

After Paul, Christianity developed in different ways in different places under different leaders. The Western churches developed the doctrine that Jesus was God, for example, while the Eastern churches did not. Doctrines and practices have continued proliferating to our own day, when there are over two thousand sects of Christianity. Here we will consider some of the teachings of the large Christian sects that are relevant to the tragic and comic visions. Some traditions, we shall see, are more tragic and others more comic.

Many of the teachings of Jesus that inclined toward the tragic or the comic vision, such as hell and heaven, continued to incline Christianity in those directions, but in the first four centuries after Jesus there were new teachings that had tragic and comic ramifications. Three important ones were (1) mind/body dualism, (2) Original Sin, and (3) the sanctioning of violence. We can consider these one at a time.

In the beginning of Christianity, fathers of the church like Tatian and Lactantius taught, as Jesus and the writers of the New Testament had, that living forever was a gift from God and not our natural fate. If Jesus had not intervened in history, human beings would naturally have all been extinguished at their death. That made the natural human condition look fairly tragic, much as it had in the late Hebrew Bible. But then Greek dualism became more influential, especially under St. Augustine. In this view, what we ordinarily call a human being is really two things, a body and a soul. The soul is the bearer of the person's identity and is separable from the body at death. Eventually, Christianity adopted this unbiblical notion, teaching that all human beings had immortal souls, even apart from Jesus' Redemption. Death was not the natural end of life, as in the Hebrew Bible; it was merely a change of state.

This Christian dualism was more optimistic than biblical monism, at least for those who would go to heaven, and in that way, was pro-comic. But in another way, dualism worked against the comic vision, by making the human body into something base, something that opposed what a human being really was, something to be transcended. That evaluation, which had started with St. Paul, was behind the championing of celibacy, Christian monasticism, and later Puritanism, all of which were anti-comic.

The second early Christian teaching with implications for the tragic and comic visions was St. Augustine's doctrine of Original Sin. While the fall of Adam was already part of the biblical heritage, Augustine added several elements to the biblical story.[15] First, the sin of Adam was interpreted as a sexual sin, so that sexuality became the basic form of fallenness and corruption. Second, it was the woman Eve who tempted Adam, so women were dangerous. Third, the sin of Adam became part of the heritage of the human race, so that all of us are born corrupted and sinful. Fourth, it is this innate corruption from which the Messiah, Jesus, redeemed us. He saved us from Original Sin, atoning for that sin so that our immortal souls can enter heaven. These ideas, now standard Christian beliefs, were not taught by Jesus, and are not found in

Judaism, Islam, or even all sects of Christianity. More importantly for our purposes, these ideas pushed Christian thinking away from the comic vision and toward the tragic vision.

Yet a third anti-comic, pro-tragic development starting with Augustine was the justification of violence. Jesus and Paul both condemned violence, telling their followers to endure mistreatment and to pray for their persecutors.[16] The first three centuries of Christians were mostly pacifists.[17] But when in the fourth-century Christianity changed from an underground religion to a mainstream religion, and then to the state religion of the Roman Empire, pacifism became inconsistent with its new political status. A pacifist empire is a contradiction in terms. To assume power in the Roman empire, and then to create the Holy Roman Empire, Christianity had to drop Jesus' pacifism and nonjudgmentalism. So Christians developed political ideologies that emphasized obedience to political authority, made it possible for Christians to serve in the army, and then rationalized Christian armies, as in the Crusades. At the same time, they created a male hierarchy that emphasized respect for authority. Over history, Christians would kill millions of people, most of them other Christians, with the blessings of Christian chaplains. All of this militarism was in direct opposition to the teachings of Jesus, and pushed Christianity away from the comic vision.

Despite all these pro-tragic features of Christianity, however, there did not develop a fully tragic vision of life in Christianity. The cardinal virtues of faith in God and his providence, and hope for eternal salvation were obviously incompatible with the tragic spirit. Christianity also discouraged the self-assertion and questioning characteristic of tragic heroes. On the cross Jesus had cried out, "My God, my God, why have you forsaken me?" (Mark 15:34; Matt. 27:46). But that moment passed quickly, and was never interpreted by Christians as tragic protest. The paradigm Christian response to suffering was always humble submission and obedience to God's will.

In Christianity, the self-concern and questioning of a tragic hero would usually be interpreted as a kind of pride, the fundamental sin in Christianity. Like the other monotheistic faiths, Christianity puts God at the center of our attention. And Christianity allows for even less questioning of God's providence than Judaism does: while the rabbis in the death camp described by Elie Wiesel could put God on trial, Christian ministers or priests doing the same thing would be guilty of blasphemy.

It is because Christianity never produced a fully tragic vision that it has never had tragic role models. In the Christian picture, those most likely to question pointless suffering would be the damned, but, they were never role models. Christians were not even supposed to pity them.

The Calvinist Vision

Despite these limitations on the development of a fully tragic vision in Christianity, a fairly tragic vision did evolve from Augustine's line of thinking. It reached its fullest development in Calvinism.

The Calvinist vision embraces Augustine's dualism and doctrine of Original Sin, and also contrasts God's sovereignty with human impotence. Unlike many Christian forms of dualism, Calvinism does not celebrate the human soul over the human body, because it sees the soul as debased along with the body. Because of Original Sin, everything about human beings is debased.

> Good men, and beyond all others Augustine, have laboured to demonstrate that we derive an innate depravity from our very birth. . . . Every descendant . . . from the impure source, is born infected with the contagion of sin: and even before we behold the light of life, we are in the sight of God defiled and polluted. . . . From a putrefied root . . . have sprung putrid branches, which have transmitted their putrescence to remoter ramifications . . . there was in Adam such a spring of corruption, that it transfused from parents to children in a perpetual stream.[18]

Because of our inherited depravity, human beings naturally tend to do only evil. "The human will is fettered by depraved and inordinate desires, so that it cannot aspire after anything that is good."[19]

> Can you except yourself from the number of those whose feet are swift to shed blood, whose hands are polluted with rapine and murder, whose throats are like open sepulchers, whose tongues are deceitful, whose lips are envenomed, whose works are useless, iniquitous, corrupt, and deadly, whose souls are estranged from God, the inmost recesses of whose hearts are full of depravity, whose eyes are insidiously employed, whose minds are elated with insolence—in a word, all whose powers are prepared for the commission of atrocious and innumerable crimes?[20]

Sometimes we perform good actions, Calvin admits. Such actions, however, are not from our own initiative, but only from God's working in us.

Because of our depravity, we all naturally deserve hell, and left to our own devices, we would all end up there. Adding to the fatalism here is Calvin's teaching that before humans are ever created, they are either elected by God for salvation, or reprobated for damnation. God's choice here is not based on merit or lack of merit, for there is no merit in anything human beings can do. Nor is there any other reason why God chooses as He does—it is simply His free choice. Of those chosen for damnation, Calvin says, "They are abandoned to this depravity because they have been raised up, by a just but inscrutable judgment of God, to display His glory in their condemnation. . . . Though we cannot comprehend the reason of this, let us be content with some degree of ignorance where the wisdom of God soars into its own sublimity."[21]

Calvin's fatalism here is stronger than that in the traditional problem of God's foreknowledge conflicting with human free choice. It is not just that God knows in advance that we will be saved or damned, but that He has chosen us to be saved or damned, and none of our own efforts could possibly save us. Indeed, whether we are saved or damned, we cannot do anything ourselves except sin. We cannot even turn to God in faith to save us, for faith is God's working in us, too.

Even Greek tragic heroes were not as fated as this. At least they had free will, something Calvin denied. While Calvin's fatalism is pro-tragic, he presents humans as so impotent that they are more like victims in melodrama than heroes in tragedy, who at least make choices, act from those choices, and are self-reliant. Tragedy also requires a certain dignity, even nobility, that we can admire—recall Aristotle's maxim that the tragic hero is better than the average person. But if no human being could strive toward good, then what could human dignity be? In the Calvinist vision, not only the damned but even the saved seem to lack human dignity. They too are totally depraved and can choose nothing good by themselves. They are saved only by God's grace. Earlier we suggested that the idea of salvation by grace was pro-comic, but in Calvinism its strong association with fatalism seems to cancel any comic overtones. Comic characters, after all, whatever their foibles and weaknesses, are not incapable of good actions.

While its denial of free will and human nobility keeps the Calvinist vision of life from being fully tragic, I think that in the fate of the damned, Calvinism presents the most tragic scenario in Christianity. To see the tragedy here, we can address the five questions in our Tragic Profile to one of the reprobated in hell.

1. *Is suffering orderly and understandable?*

The suffering in life is said to be punishment for sin, but humans are created unable to refrain from sinning, so it is hard to understand how it could be fair for God to punish them. And what purpose could punishment serve? It is hard to see how it could be retribution. Could a just God demand retribution for unavoidable actions motivated by the nature with which He created humans? Nor does punishment reform sinners—they are as unable to do anything good of their own accord after punishment as before.

When we turn from suffering on earth to the suffering of the damned, the unintelligibility of suffering gets worse. Reform in hell is impossible, of course, and even if it made sense to demand retribution for unavoidable offenses, surely the punishment should not be infinitely greater than the offense, as hell is. And if one of the damned asks the larger question, "Why me?" the answer is that God freely chose— for no reason at all—that some would be damned and some saved. That makes the ultimate suffering of hell random, and so neither orderly nor understandable, just as it makes the opposite, salvation and heaven, random.

2. *Is suffering avoidable?*

In Calvinism, suffering follows from human sin. Since sin is not avoidable, neither is suffering, including the ultimate suffering of hell.

3. *Does suffering always at least have the potential to bring about some greater good, or is some suffering pointless?*

According to Calvin, God's condemnation and punishment of some people "displays His glory," but even if we consider that a good, it is hard to see what greater *human* good suffering brings about? And when we consider the endless suffering of hell, there is clearly no greater human good served. Hell is the ultimate in pointless suffering.

4. *Will everything work out for the best in the end?*

No, for the damned, everything will work out for the worst, and that condition will last forever.

5. *How should we react to suffering?*

Calvin does not have advice for the damned, of course. But we can imagine their reacting to their suffering with classic tragic defiance.

The Calvinist vision, then, comes close to the classic tragic vision, stopping short only because it denies human autonomy and dignity. In that way, it presents human life as worse than even the tragic vision does. We are all depraved from birth and so too worthless to be tragic!

The Franciscan Vision

Having seen how far Christianity went toward the tragic vision, we can now look at opposing comic developments in Christianity. Alongside the Puritans and their ilk, there have always been Christians with comic sensibility. The number has often been small, at least since Christianity became politically powerful in the fourth century; but in the last half-century it has flowered, and if Christian thinkers like Harvey Cox and Conrad Hyers are right, it offers us something of unique value. Cox has said that the comic vision "supplies the only possible idiom for faith at a time of dead gods, museum churches, and antiquarian theology."[22]

There is next to nothing about comedy or humor in the thousands of books of Christian theology. Thomas Aquinas mentions laughter's relation to rationality a few times. Karl Barth's twelve-volume *Church Dogmatics* gives about a page to humor's connection with humility.[23] But if we collected all the books of Christian theology, excised the handful of pages that even mentioned humor, and sent the collection to Mars, Martian readers would never figure out that the human race was capable of laughter.

Several times in history, church officials have condemned laughter and comedy. When the Puritans came to power in England, they outlawed comedy. Some monastic orders had rules prohibiting laughter. St. John Chrysostom had this advice:

> To laugh, to speak jocosely, does not seem an acknowledged sin, but it leads to acknowledged sin. Thus laughter often gives birth to foul discourse, and foul discourse to actions still more foul. Often from words and laughter proceed railing and insult; and from railing, and insult, blows and wounds; and from blows and wounds, slaughter and murder. If, then, thou wouldst take good counsel for thyself, avoid not merely foul words, and foul deeds, or blows, and wounds, and murders, but unseasonable laughter, itself.[24]

Despite such attacks on laughter, Harvey Cox has suggested that the comic spirit is natural to Christianity and may have flourished in its first three centuries, when Christians were social outcasts. As Christianity became the state religion of the Roman Empire, however, its comic spirit was suppressed.[25] One of the earliest representations of Christ in the catacombs, Cox points out, is of a crucified human figure with the head of a donkey. There may have been non-comic symbolism here, of course, but "it might also be true that those catacomb Christians had a deeper sense of the comic absurdity of their position than we think they did. A wretched band of slaves, derelicts, and square pegs, they must have sensed occasionally how ludicrous their claims appeared."[26]

To Cox's suggestion that Christianity's comic spirit was suppressed in the fourth century, we could draw a parallel with Christian pacifism, which was also squelched as Christianity came to political power. But just as Christian pacifism did not disappear, neither did the comic spirit. The Greek church, in fact, still has the ancient custom of setting aside the day after Easter as a day of laughter, even within the sanctuary, because of the big joke God has played on Satan in resurrecting Jesus. The sixth-century Greek church also developed a Holy Fool tradition, based on Paul's idea that Christians are fools for Christ's sake, in which acting like a clown was an expression of piety.

Even in the Western church, the comic spirit was never eliminated. In medieval times, the liturgy was sometimes accompanied by "mystery plays" enacting events from the Bible. From them developed modern comedy and tragedy, and they had comic moments. In one part of the York cycle, for example, the soldiers are embarrassed to discover that in preparing the cross for Jesus, they have bored the holes wrong so that Jesus' body will not fit.[27] Medieval Christian literature also had Dante's *Divine Comedy*. But the most striking evidence of the comic spirit in medieval Christianity were three festivals occurring after Christmas, on the days of the old Roman Saturnalia: Holy Innocent's Day, the Feast of Asses, and the Feast of Fools. On Holy Innocent's Day, a young boy replaced the bishop. The Feast of Fools began during the singing of the Magnificat on the Feast of the Circumcision. At the words "He has put down the mighty from their seat and has exalted the humble and the meek," young clergy drove the senior clergy from the church. Then they put on masks, converted the altar into a banquet table, and performed a parody of the Holy Mass. Sometimes a donkey was brought into the sanctuary as an incarnation of the Lord of Disorder.[28]

The person who best embodied the comic spirit of medieval Western Christianity was St. Francis of Assisi (1181–1226). After a series of religious experiences as a young man, Francis dedicated his life to imitating Jesus' life and work, something he did with exuberance. For him, all creatures reflected God and the simplest daily events were cause for celebration. He called animals and even the moon and sun "Sister" and "Brother." His own body was "Brother Ass." In imitation of Jesus, Francis lived a life of charity. Poverty was his "Bride" and "Lady." His selflessness was not based on feelings of worthlessness, depravity, or guilt, but on a healthy sense of humor about himself.

Francis' love of life, his playfulness, and his charity were immensely appealing. In his short life, he attracted thousands of followers. Within two years of his death, he was canonized. But as the Middle Ages came to a close, the comic spirit in Christianity seemed to wane again. At the Council of Basel in 1431, the Church condemned the Feast of Fools. With the Protestant Reformation and the Catholic Counter-Reformation of the next century, the comic spirit seemed to hit a low in Christian history. In the following centuries up to our own, Harvey Cox says, capitalism and the Industrial Revolution have squelched the spirit of festivity and fantasy that foster the comic vision of life. The medieval calendar had dozens of major festival days, occasions of public play and celebration; we are down to a handful of holidays, and most of those involve no public play or celebration. Festivity and playfulness have been supplanted by the work ethic, and in the process, the Franciscan vision has seriously declined.

In the last thirty years, however, there has been a significant revival of the comic spirit within certain Christian groups. In the 1960s Pope John XXIII let some fresh air into the tradition-bound Catholic Church with his *aggiornamento* (updating of the church) and Second Vatican Council. Catholics began singing new songs, accompanied by guitars instead of pipe organs. Banners and posters appeared in sanctuaries. Sister Corita Kent made one for Christmas that said: "He cared enough to send the very best."[29] Father John Naus, S.J., a philosophy professor at Marquette University, began his work, or rather play, as Tumbleweed the Clown in 1971. Protestant churches were even more experimental in bringing festivity into church services. Not only folk music, but jazz and rock could be heard: some churches had dance and multimedia events. At the 1966 World's Fair in New York, the Protestant Pavilion featured a movie in which the Christ figure appeared as a circus clown. Several churches since then have established clown ministries. In 1986 a group of Protestant and Catholic humorists, comedians, cartoonists, and clowns came together to form the Fellowship of Merry Christians. Its publication *The Joyful Noiseletter* appeared on April 1 of that year and has been growing in circulation ever since. The Fellowship's members now include hundreds of clergy from dozens of denominations.

Behind these changes is a rethinking of Christianity. Beginning in the mid-1960s with Elton Trueblood's *The Humor of Christ*, there have been a number of books arguing that the Christian vision of life is a comic vision. Among the seminal thinkers here are Harvey Cox, with *The Feast of Fools*, and Conrad Hyers, with his anthology *Holy Laughter*, followed by several books.

Those who argue that Christianity has a comic vision share some general features. One is that they do not emphasize orthodoxy and sectarian divisions, but are likely to be highly ecumenical. They especially do not emphasize the pro-tragic/anti-comic doctrines of Original Sin, mind-body dualism, and hell. On the positive side, they embrace creation in all its diversity and disorder. Like comedy in general, they love the world "warts and all." Creation comes from God, and though imperfect, is basically good. Humans are made in God's image, and while they often fall short of their good intentions, they are not depraved.

In Christians with a comic vision, the goodness of the world and its Creator evokes joy and celebration. They hold that festivity and play are as essential to life as work is, that human beings need aesthetic moments as well as practical moments. This aesthetic dimension has always been found in sacraments and other religious rituals, but proponents of the comic Christian vision look for it in all of life. Imagination should not be suppressed by religion, but stimulated. The best expression of this idea is part 2 of Harvey Cox's *The Feast of Fools*.

Religions like Zen that lack the religious/nonreligious distinction are more comic, and in Christian comic visions there is little distinction between the religious and nonreligious. They especially reject the idea of a sacred realm where laughter and delight are out of bounds.

In Christian comic visions not only is this life good, but people are on their way to a better one in heaven, and heaven will have several comic features. For one, as we have seen, heaven is a gift of God rather than something earned. Secondly, heaven is a state of play, not of work. And thirdly, heaven provides a comic twist to this life, turning around whatever misfortunes we have experienced on earth. Because of heaven, the Christian can take setbacks in stride, like a comic protagonist. As Elton Trueblood wrote, commenting on G. K. Chesterton, those who had come to know Christ "might be sad about the little things, but were tumultuously gay about the big things."[30] There are still moments of suffering and sadness, to be sure, but life is not a tragedy, because it has the ultimate happy ending. Northrup Frye put it this way, "From the point of view of Christianity . . . tragedy is an episode in that larger scheme of redemption and resurrection to which Dante gave the name of *commedia*. . . . The sense of tragedy as a prelude to comedy is hardly separable from anything explicitly Christian."[31] In the last forty years Christian churches have emphasized the Resurrection, thus, hope. Catholics, for example, have gotten rid of the black vestments for the funeral Mass, which is now called the Mass of the Resurrection.

Another important part of Christian comic visions can be found in their ethics. What should guide our lives is Jesus' spirit of love for God and for all human beings. The virtues advocated by the comic vision are those taught by Jesus: tolerance, nonjudgmentalism, nonviolence, and forgiveness. Given this overlap, it is surprising how few theologians have seen humor's connection with Christian virtues. Reinhold Niebuhr is one of those few. He points out that "the ability to laugh at oneself is the prelude to the sense of contrition.

Laughter is a vestibule to the temple of confession."[32] Conrad Hyers explains that "Humility includes the ability to laugh at oneself and the refusal to take oneself too seriously. Laughter may open the way to forgiveness, for in laughter hostilities are softened, just as forgiveness allows enemies to laugh together. Repentance ends in laughter, and repentance needs laughter to preserve itself from moroseness and self-chastisement."[33]

Humor is especially useful in getting people to see themselves and everything in their lives with emotional disengagement, from a higher, more objective perspective. They can poke fun at themselves, and at the traditions and authorities they follow. They think flexibly and critically, even iconoclastically, as Jesus did. As Reinhold Niebuhr said, "Both humour and faith are expressions of the freedom of the human spirit, of its capacity to stand outside of life, and itself, and view the whole scene."[34]

In *The Feast of Fools*, Harvey Cox calls on Christians to put the festivity back into their religion in order to cure "our cultural sickness—our worship of work and production, and our insensitivity to the mystery from which human history arises and toward which it inevitably flows."[35] Cox even proposes a new icon for Christianity in his last chapter, "Christ the Harlequin":

> Christ has come to previous generations in various guises, as teacher, as judge, as healer. In today's world these traditional images of Christ have lost much of their power. Now in a new, or really an old but recaptured guise, Christ has made an unexpected entrance onto the stage of modern secular life. Enter Christ the harlequin: The personification of festivity and fantasy in an age that had almost lost both. Coming now in greasepaint and halo, this Christ is able to touch our jaded modern consciousness as other images of Christ cannot.[36]

Islam

In exploring Christianity, we noted that the New Testament was more unified than the Hebrew Bible, because it was written by fewer people over a shorter period of time. The scripture of Islam, the Qur'an, is even more unified than the New Testament, because it was dictated by one person, the Prophet Muhammad, over some twenty-two years, and was compiled soon after his death. More than in the other two monotheistic religions, revelation in Islam is a single document with a single message.

When Islam arose in the seventh century, there were many religions in the Arab and Persian world—Judaism, Christianity, Zoroastrianism, and various polytheisms. Muhammad saw the culture around him as licentious and debased; even the monotheists had strayed from following the will of God. His central message was that there is only one God and we need to submit to his will. "Islam" means submission. But submission is not passivity—we need to be active, especially in bringing about a just society on earth.

Judaism and Christianity were on the right track with their monotheism, Muhammad taught, and both the Hebrew Bible and the New Testament were revelations from God, but misunderstandings had arisen in these religions. Islam accepted the Biblical story that Abraham had received a call from God, but rejected the claim of Judaism that God intended his religion for a single ethnic group. It accepted Christianity's claim that God had sent Jesus, and that at the end of the world there would be a Last Judgment followed by heaven and hell, but it rejected as idolatrous the Christian teaching that Jesus was God. It also rejected the doctrines that humans are born with Original Sin, and that Jesus had redeemed the human race from Original Sin.

Most of the basic teachings of Islam are already in Judaism, Christianity, or both, as are the features of Islam that incline it toward and away from the tragic and comic visions. But Islam has its own configuration of these teachings and features.

One feature of Islam shared with Christianity that inclines it toward the tragic vision and away from the comic vision is its teaching about hell.

Like Christianity and early Judaism, too, Islam is influenced by militarism. Its early years were filled with military campaigns, and ever since, its central virtues have been those of the warrior: courage, singleness of purpose, submission to authority, and loyalty. Dignity and honor are central. Life is a struggle in which we engage in *jihad*, crusades, with unbelievers and idolators, and with forces within ourselves. Islam has never preached pacifism as Jesus did. Indeed, retribution is expected: a freeman is to be killed to avenge the murder of a freeman, a slave for a slave, and so forth.

This militarism in Islam is part of a wider pattern of patriarchy. Although the Qur'an talks of women's equality with men, Muslim cultures have always given ruling power to men, and women have had to obey their husbands. According to a traditional understanding of the Last Judgment, men will be judged by how they submitted to God, while women will be judged by how they submitted to their husbands.

Patriarchal thinking in Islam shows clearly in the perception of Muhammad himself. Though he was just a man, he has been treated as the perfect role model. Thousands of *hadith*—stories about Muhammad's life from outside the Qur'an—have been collected and used as a source of Islamic law. What Muhammad did and did not do is taken to be binding even in matters such as whether to eat onions, shave, or use a brush to clean one's teeth.

Islam's militarism and patriarchy indicate a general lack of mental flexibility, which can also be seen in other protragic, anti-comic traits. One is a respect for authority and tradition that leaves little room for critical or creative thinking. Another is a low tolerance for disorder. Muhammad's emphasis on God's law came from his disgust toward what he saw as the licentiousness of his culture. For Muslims ever since, the highest human pursuit has been the clarification and administration of God's law.

More generally, the moral ideal in Islam is obedience to God. Our purpose in living is not to work out our own destinies, but to submit to kismet, the destiny that God has chosen for us. Whether we experience joy or suffering, Muslims say, "Ma sh'Allah," it is God's will.

Although the Qur'an teaches that God does not change in a people what they do not change in themselves, belief in kismet obviously calls human free will into question. But while many Christian thinkers have thought it necessary to find some compatibility between divine predetermination and free will, orthodox Muslim thinkers have been happy to give up the idea that humans have free will. If such freedom existed, they have sometimes argued, it would limit the freedom of God.

Despite its mental rigidity and other pro-tragic traits, however, Islam does not go all the way to a tragic vision of life. It shows some mental flexibility, as in its acceptance of Jews and Christians, and its sanctioning of four schools of law. Even the fatalism of kismet does not by itself entail a tragic vision, at least for the righteous. Their fate is the Garden, heaven; their lives will have a happy ending.

Islam also lacks the questioning of, and protest against suffering, which characterize the tragic vision. It has nothing like the Book of Job, nor even the despairing cry of Jesus, "My God, my God, why have you forsaken me?" What Christian philosophers call the Problem of Evil does not arise in Islam. There is complete confidence in God, and so no questioning "Why me?" when suffering comes along. Even Shi'ite Muslims, whose history is marked by persecution and whose rituals include many commemorations of martyrs and their suffering, do not have a tragic attitude toward their suffering. It is part of their struggle, and in the end, God will compensate them for it in heaven.

To see how Islam embraces only some of the tragic vision, we can raise the questions in our Tragic Profile.

1. *Is suffering orderly and understandable?*

In Islam all events, including all instances of suffering, fit into the master plan of the provident God. Humans can understand how some suffering serves God's purposes. With suffering whose purpose we cannot figure out, we simply confess ignorance and say, "Ma sh'Allah"—It is God's will. This resignation to God's will makes any further questioning moot.

2. *Is suffering avoidable?*

No, because all events are willed by God.

3. *Does suffering always at least have the potential to bring about some greater good, or is some suffering pointless?*

All suffering has the potential to bring about some greater good in God's plan. For God, no suffering is pointless.

4. *Will everything work out for the best in the end?*

From God's perspective, again, everything will work out. Islam does not raise the question from the perspective of the damned.

5. *How should we react to suffering?*

Ma sh'Allah, it is God's will. There is no room for questioning or protesting God's will. We should surrender our lives into God's hands, realizing that suffering can have a purifying effect on us.

Islam stops well short of a fully tragic vision. It even has one major pro-comic feature, its thoroughly social vision of life. Like Judaism, it emphasizes the family and the community, and rejects a celibate or monastic life. Islam teaches the equality of all human beings, who, the Qur'an says, are as alike as the teeth in a comb. And despite the sexist treatment Muslim women have sometimes endured in patriarchal society, the Qur'an is the only monotheistic scripture that claims equality for women and sets out their rights. Islam also champions the poor and the weak. According to one tradition, the Prophet said that the poor shall enter paradise five hundred years before the rich. Almsgiving is one of its Five Pillars, and its tax codes and social legislation prescribe caring for widows, orphans, the poor, travelers, and slaves. Islam also stresses political engagement. All people should participate in decision-making and work for social justice.

This egalitarian social vision in Islam does not take it very far toward the comic vision, however, mostly because of Islam's overall solemnity and lack of playfulness. In the comic vision, not only do we interact as equals, but there is occasion for festivity in our interactions. We take pleasure in each other's company through music, singing, dancing, and sharing food and drink. In Islam, by contrast, life is fundamentally solemn. Because Muhammad wanted to overcome the licentiousness of his society and get everyone to follow God's laws, he took a puritanical attitude toward play, festivity, and pleasure. There are only two major celebrations in the Islamic year, the Breaking of the Fast at the end of Ramadan, the month of fasting; and the Feast of the Sacrifice, which commemorates Abraham's agreeing to sacrifice his son. Socializing at these and other times is mostly visiting and sharing food with family.

Standard Islam uses no religious music or singing. Men and women dancing together is *haram*, forbidden. Even single-sex folk dancing, and music in some Muslim societies, are discouraged. Drinking alcohol is declared *haram* in the Qur'an.

In most religions, one of the standard occasions for festivity is the wedding, but in Islam a wedding consists of the negotiation of the marriage contract, including a pre-nuptial agreement regarding what the wife will receive if the husband divorces her. In different cultures, Muslims add various nonreligious ceremonies to the wedding, but the wedding itself is just the drawing up of the contract.

Besides this lack of festivity, there are no comic role models like Francis of Assisi in standard Islam, nor the pro-comic ethic of love. In Islam, God is not "Our Father," and what we are commanded is to submit to His will. Although Muslims are taught to try to please God, there is no emphasis on the love of God. The Christian ideas of grace and vicarious salvation, which are also pro-comic, do not occur in Islam. Heaven is not a gift from God, but something we earn.

With its solemnity and emphasis on submission, Islam has never sanctioned anything like the Holy Fool tradition, the Feast of Asses and Feast of Fools, or other forms of iconoclasm. The few Sufi mystics who did poke fun at the standard traditions were condemned.

So from the perspective of the tragic and comic visions, Islam comes down pretty much to simply monotheism as outlined in the beginning of this chapter. That monotheism has almost nothing comic about it. It does have solemnity and gravity about life, and some elements of the tragic vision, such as fatalism. But because it does not allow questioning or protest, or even self-concern about suffering, it does not embrace the tragic vision of life.

Conclusions

In our examination of Eastern religions, we found almost no tendency toward the tragic vision and a considerable tendency toward the comic vision. In Western religions, we have found more of a range.

Within Judaism, we found some comic elements in the early Bible, but then a growing tragic vision in the later Bible. The last two millennia of Judaism have done little to change the direction of that movement. The Holocaust seems to eliminate the possibility of the comic vision from Judaism.

Christianity, by contrast, emerged from persecution after just a few centuries to become the dominant religion of Europe, and so it lacked the earthly pessimism of its parent, Judaism. It also offered the hope of eternal happiness, so it lacked much of the tragic inclination of Judaism. Although its teaching about hell made it tragic for the damned, its vision of life for the saved had many comic elements. As Christianity evolved into thousands of sects, some went in comic directions, which we have described collectively as the Franciscan vision. But sects embracing Platonic dualism and the doctrine of Original Sin went in tragic directions, culminating in Calvinism.

Islam, with its total submission to God, has neither the individualism and questioning of suffering required for the tragic vision, nor the playfulness of the comic vision.

Chapter 8

New Religions

$\mathcal{W}$e have examined comic and tragic aspects of the major world religions. But the birth of religions did not stop with Islam in the seventh century, of course, or with Protestantism in the sixteenth. New religions and new sects of the major traditions continued to develop, and are still developing in our own century. In the thirty years after World War II, some three thousand new religions appeared in the United States, and eight hundred in Western Europe.[1] In the last thirty years, as mainline Christian churches have lost members, new religions have grown. To make our exploration of the comic and tragic aspects of religions more complete, we should consider the new religions of the last century.

Many new religions are responses to modernity, especially to the alienation and moral disorientation common in industrial cultures. In helping people find their place in the world, new religions draw from diverse religious and nonreligious sources, especially psychology and philosophy. Most new religions develop in urban areas, which are crossroads for ideas from different cultures and different disciplines, and so syncretism is common.

Since North America has had the largest number of new religions, we shall focus our attention there, though most of our comments would also apply to new religions in Western Europe and Japan. For our purposes we can divide new religions into two main groups: the self-oriented therapeutic religions, which we can call "religions of the self," and the authoritarian religions.

Religions of the Self

The religions of the self celebrate not a god on high, but something within oneself. One group calls itself simply P.S.I., "People Seeking Inside." These religions arise from three main sources. The first is Eastern traditions brought to North America. From Hinduism, for example, come the Transcendental Meditation movement of Maharishi Mahesh Yogi, the International Society for Krishna Consciousness of Swami Prabhupada, Eckankar, the Divine Light Mission, the Rajneesh Foundation, and, more recently, the books of Deepak Chopra.

The second source of religions of the self is the American idealist tradition that began in the nineteenth century with American Transcendentalism and New Thought. In the twentieth century this trend developed further in "human potential" movements such as Positive Thinking and humanistic psychology. In both centuries American idealism has been linked with mental and physical healing, as in New Thought, Silva Mind Control, est (Erhart Seminar Training), and many New Age movements.

American idealism and Eastern traditions are not completely independent. Ralph Waldo Emerson and other American transcendentalists were fond of Indian thought. Several new religions have embraced Hindu ideas, especially the idea that reality is ultimately mental, and that suffering and evil arise from incorrect perceptions of the world. The goal of many new movements is like *moksha* in Hinduism: they seek enlightenment—liberation from bondage to an unhealthy perspective.

The third source of American religions of the self is the romantic desire to restore the natural world to its rightful place in human life, and to bring back pretechnological imagination and enchantment. From this desire have come witchcraft and other forms of neopaganism celebrating the natural world and connecting humans to it through astrology, divination, and magic.

Authoritarian Religions

Our second category, new authoritarian religions, includes two kinds, revivalist sects of old religions like Christianity, and what are popularly known as cults. In both there is a patriarchal human leader and usually a patriarchal divinity.

Revivalist sects include most of the evangelical, pentecostal, and fundamentalist movements of the last thirty years. They are usually founded by a charismatic patriarch, who combines traditional ideas and rituals with some new ones, and presents the package in an appealing way, usually with a message of urgency.

Cults are also typically built on a selection of traditional and new ideas and rituals, but here charismatic leaders are even more important. When the public thinks of a cult, they think of its patriarch—the Rev. Sun Myung Moon of the Unification Church, the Rev. Jim Jones of the People's Temple, David Koresh of the Branch Davidians, and Do (Marshall Herff Applewhite) of Heaven's Gate. The central feature of cults is not their ideology, which is usually derived from standard beliefs, but the blind obedience and total commitment they require of followers. The mass suicide of the Jonestown and the Heaven's Gate cults shows how far blind obedience to a patriarch can go. Typically these groups are not even called cults until their leaders command them to do something that brings them into conflict with mainstream society. When the Rev. Jim Jones and his People's Temple were living peacefully with their neighbors in Indiana and California, for example, they were known as a small Christian sect. But when outsiders complained that Jones was brainwashing his followers and taking their money, and especially after he moved the whole group to South America, where he later ordered a mass suicide, they were called a cult.

While the authoritarianism of revivalist sects may not be as overwhelming as the authoritarianism of cults, it is strong. In fundamentalist Christianity, for example, there is no celebration of the self or autonomy, and living a good life consists of obeying a patriarchal God.

No Tragic Vision in New Religions

With this basic understanding of new religions, we can now examine them in light of the comic and tragic visions. The first thing to notice is that the tragic vision does not emerge in either the religions of the self or the authoritarian religions.

Religions of the self usually deny basic tenets of tragedy—that evil is a fundamental feature of the world, for example, which is beyond our control. Instead of believing that chance events ruin us, these religions see evil as a product of the way we think. We can control our perceptions and attitudes, and so control our destiny. Many of the new religions of the self, in fact, teach that we can become whatever we set our mind to becoming: the world is ideoplastic. Seichō no Ie (House of Growth), a Japanese religion incorporating ideas from American New Thought, teaches that all things are perfect and spiritual; there is no matter, suffering, or evil; and we may eliminate any problem through the power of mind. In such an optimistic view everything can be under our control, suffering is not a problem, and so the tragic vision cannot get a foothold.

Authoritarian new religions do not typically teach that the world is mind-dependent, and many of them have pro-tragic features such as militarism, patriarchalism, and simplistic ideologies. Still, none embraces a tragic worldview. The basic reason is practical. In order to grow, a new religion must entice people away from their current religions, and so it must present itself as more attractive than those religions. Incorporating the tragic vision into a new religion would be counterproductive here, because it would bring bad news rather than good news, reducing the religion's attractiveness. That may also explain why in this century the tragic vision has declined in the major religions.

New authoritarian religions do bring up the problematic side of life; indeed, many have apocalyptic visions in which catastrophe is imminent. But these religions go on to offer salvation and liberation—they tell us what we can do to escape. It is this pairing of an urgent problem with a solution that makes these religions attractive, especially when that solution is available only to members of their group, and is fairly easy. The offer of cosmic hope blocks the tragic vision.

The Comic Vision in Religions of the Self

If neither kind of new religion is tragic, is either comic? The answer is that while the new authoritarian religions, like the old ones, are not comic, the new religions of the self, like the old, show tendencies toward the comic vision. Here we can consider eight pro-comic features in new religions of the self:

The Power of Mind

A major theme of religions of the self is that consciousness influences or even constitutes our world. In weak forms this mentalism says merely that thinking positive thoughts will make our experiences more positive. Dale Carnegie courses and the self-esteem movement are examples. In a stronger form in Hindu idealism and related Western teachings, mentalism says that my consciousness is what I really am, that my soul is a spiritual being without beginning or end, and even that my soul *is* the ultimate reality—atman is Brahman. We ordinarily distinguish between the self as a subject of consciousness and the world as an object of consciousness, of course, but the ultimate truth is that the world *is* my consciousness. The world I may think of as standing on its own is actually, like my dreams, a world constituted by my consciousness.

An important forerunner of today's mentalism was Phineas Quimby, the founder of New Thought and teacher of Mary Baker Eddy, the founder of Christian Science. Quimby bridged the metaphysical gap between God and human beings from both directions: God is immanent in the world, he taught, and humans have a divine nature. Indeed, the whole universe is spiritual. Evil is not a force independent of our minds, but a product of thinking incorrectly. In this approach, as in Christian Science today, healing, indeed correcting any problem, is accomplished through thinking.

In contrast to religions of the self, authoritarian religions do not celebrate the individual's consciousness, and certainly would never identify it with ultimate reality. In these religions, in fact, the perspective and desires of the self are suspect, usually because human beings are seen as fallen creatures. Whatever needs to be done we should ask God to help us achieve—by ourselves we are nothing and can do nothing. We should not celebrate our consciousness, but suppress it in submission to the divine or human patriarch.

The emphasis on the power of mind in the religions of the self can be seen as pro-comic, just as the suppression of the individual's consciousness in authoritarian religions can be seen as anti-comic. Comedy's goal is amusement, an enjoyable shift in consciousness. The punchline of a joke or the dénouement of a comic scene typically works by making us change our perspective quickly to see things in a new way. "Getting it" is a kind of enlightenment, on a smaller scale than *moksha*, to be sure, but still enlightenment.

Moreover, we can enjoy shifts of consciousness not only with comedy, but in our everyday experience. Those with comic vision shift their perspective often, especially from close-up, practical positions to distanced, playful positions. From those disengaged perspectives, they enjoy incongruous experiences that would otherwise be disturbing.

The new religions of the self share with the comic vision at least the idea that our perspective determines our experience, especially whether it will be positive or negative. Those religions that follow classical Hinduism in claiming that the common sense phenomenal world is illusory are more comic still in making all of ordinary experience *maya*, a kind of grand joke; getting the joke will be our liberation.

Relativism

Because of their emphasis on the power of the individual mind, religions of the self tend toward conceptual and ethical relativism. They treat concepts and values not as absolute and for the universe, but as relative to persons and situations.

These religions have no lists of orthodox beliefs and commandments.

Relativism is a pro-comic feature, as we saw earlier, and its absence in authoritarian religions is an anti-comic feature. Authoritarian religions have a single standard for truth and value, such as the mind of God, and so reject either cognitive or moral relativism. As in the older monotheistic religions, discovering the truth is coming to see things the way the authority sees them, and doing what is right is obeying the authority figure.

The relativism of new religions of the self leads to other pro-comic features like pluralism and tolerance. Inversely, because the new authoritarian religions see themselves as right in both senses—knowing the truth and being moral—they present themselves not as an option, but as the only acceptable path. Rather than mere enthusiasm, they have missionary zeal. Unlike the pluralism and tolerance of the new religions of the self, they show the self-righteousness and even fanaticism of zealots.

Pragmatism

Linked with relativism in the new religions of the self is pragmatism. As in the comic vision, both thought and action are judged not in relation to some absolute standard, but in relation to whether they work for the individual thinker and agent. Not only should people "do their own thing," to use the 1960s cliche, but they should think their own way. Personal satisfaction is the touchstone for beliefs and actions. "It works for me" serves as an all-purpose justification.

Embracing of Ambiguity

With their relativism and pragmatism, the new religions of the self are comfortable with the multiplicity of diverse interpretations possible for any situation. They tend to welcome metaphor, imagination, and divergent thinking. The new authoritarian religions, on the other hand, believe in context-free truth and tend to hold that there is one correct interpretation for any situation—in monothestic fundamentalism, for example, the interpretation of the omniscient God.

Tolerance for Mistakes

Unlike traditional monotheistic religions, and unlike authoritarian new religions, the new religions of the self tend to treat
mistakes as matters of the intellect rather than the will.
Doing wrong, like being wrong, is seen not as sin committed
against God because of a depraved will, but as misjudgment,
seeing things in unhelpful ways. There is no reviling people
for their actions to get them to feel ashamed and guilty.
Rather, as in the comic vision generally, there is a tolerance
for mistakes, and wrongdoers get another chance.

Reincarnation

In most new religions of the self, the tolerance for mistakes
extends beyond this life, for they believe in reincarnation and
karma. People who have not reached a fulfilled state in this
lifetime will be born again for another try. This pro-comic
idea is rejected by most new authoritarian religions, which
teach that each person gets a single chance at life.

Aesthetic Emphasis

Related to the emphasis on the power of mind and the
embracing of ambiguity in the new religions of the self is an
aesthetic concern. Like artists, followers of many new religions are looking for ways to express their emotions and to be
creative. In Japan, the Perfect Liberty group teaches that "Life
is art, to be lived in a balanced, creative, aesthetically expres-
sive way."

People often choose new religions for their aesthetic
appeal as much as anything else. Many of these religions pub-
lish lavishly illustrated books. In a beautifully designed, ani-
mated web site on the Internet, Eckankar promotes itself as
"The Religion of the Light and Sound of God." Movements as
different as Krishna consciousness and Santeria use colorful
garments, drumming, and dancing to make rituals emotionally satisfying, memorable, and even fun. New Age movements are well known for their crystals and music. The recent
interest in angels has sparked a whole industry in jewelry and
other crafts, as well as in publishing.

The aesthetic emphasis in the new religions of the self is pro-comic since the comic vision of life emphasizes enjoyment. New authoritarian religions, by contrast, tend to have an anti-comic suspicion of pleasure and fun.

Emphasis on the Feminine

In the old patriarchal religions, and in the new authoritarian religions, the deities and the human leaders are all male. Along with this sexism go other anti-comic traits such as militarism. Most new religions of the self treat the sexes more equally. Deities and leaders can be female. In the United States even Buddhism has given positions of leadership to women. Wicca has goddesses along with gods; cults of the Goddess can dispense with males entirely.

Neopaganism as a Comic New Religion

Having seen some general pro-comic features of the new religions of the self, we can now examine a specific religious tradition in more detail. Many of the religions we have mentioned are adaptations of Eastern religions, especially Hinduism, and their pro-comic features are predictably similar to the pro-comic features of the parent religion. So for our detailed examination of a new religion, let us consider not a development of an established tradition, but a thoroughly new movement of this century, Neopaganism.

Neopaganism is not a single sect, but a number of groups attempting to bring back the religions of pre-Christian tribal Europe.[2] There are few historical records about pre-Christian tribal religions, however, and so Neopagans have had to invent beliefs, myths, rituals, ethics, and social structures. In the process, they have created several thousand new religions.

While Neopagan beliefs are diverse, five are widely accepted:

1. The supernatural is imminent in nature, rather than above nature as in standard Western monotheism.
2. Human beings are able to interact with the supernatural and have it affect their lives.

3. The supernatural is not exclusively male: it may appear as either masculine or feminine, or as neither.
4. Humans are reincarnated.
5. There is universal balance in nature.

The largest and most familiar Neopagan religion in the United States is Wicca, or witchcraft. According to a survey by Scott Russell, about half of the Neopagans in the United States claim to be Wiccan.

Besides the five metaphysical beliefs already stated, Wiccans have five moral principles. The first is called the Wiccan Rede: "And it harm none, do what you will."[3] More motivation for not hurting anyone is provided in the second principle, the Threefold Law of Retribution: what you do to someone else will be returned to you three times. The third principle is that pleasure, especially sexual pleasure, is good and to be embraced by consenting adults. Fourth, knowledge is power. And fifth, magic should be used to better oneself and the world.

In chapter 4 we contrasted the comic and tragic visions of life on twenty points, and in chapter 5 we schematized those contrasts into pro-comic and pro-tragic features of religions. If we analyze Neopaganism on those twenty points, we can see that it is overwhelmingly comic.

Under the cognitive psychology of the comic and tragic visions, we noted that the comic vision embodies mental flexibility while the tragic vision embodies mental rigidity. There we presented twelve contrasts. On eleven of these, Neopaganism comes out on the comic side.

Complex Rather Than Simple Conceptual Schemes

Neopagans are free to create their own belief systems, and there are many accounts of the supernatural to choose from. Individuals' spiritual ideas are likely to be unique sets drawn from several traditions and from their own thinking, and those sets are likely to change over time. So Neopaganism has a built-in diversity and complexity.

High Rather Than Low Tolerance for Disorder

The idea that there are many ways in which to understand the world and many ways to accomplish things allows for a high tolerance of disorder. With no absolute truth or absolute order as a goal, Neopagans are free to work and play with a wide variety of others.

Seeking Out the Unfamiliar over Preference for the Familiar

Because Neopagan religions are in the minority and are not well-accepted in America, those who have left mainstream religions for Neopaganism have had to seek out the unfamiliar. Neopagan beliefs and rituals, too, are full of the exotic and esoteric.

High Rather Than Low Tolerance for Ambiguity

Rejecting absolute truth, Neopagans are not locked into single perspectives on any issue but are free to adopt whatever perspective they find appealing or helpful. What they believe one day, they may not believe another day. The amenability of anything to many interpretations is accepted as part of the richness of human life.

Divergent over Convergent Thinking

Without a single correct perspective to achieve, Neopagans are free to think imaginatively. As a group, they tend to be quite creative. Because they lack a written tradition and archaeological information about pre-Christian European religions, as mentioned before, they have had to create most of their religions from scratch. New symbols have been invented and ancient symbols like the pentagram have been given a number of meanings.[4]

Critical Thinking over Uncritical Thinking

Joining a Neopagan group is not easy, for it requires breaking away from mainstream beliefs and rituals to embrace those frowned upon by American society at large. The Wiccan idea that we are allowed to do anything as long as we are hurting no one, for example, clashes with the divine will ethics of Western religions, and has evoked vilification from mainstream religions. The Neopagan critique of technological consumer culture also brings it into conflict with American society. On these and other basic beliefs, Neopaganism requires people to think critically.

Willingness to Change One's Mind, over Stubbornness

Without orthodoxy, Neopagans are free to change their minds on all kinds of issues. Changing one's views is seen as part of learning and growing, and so as essential to the human adventure.

Pragmatism over Idealism

Neopagan religions do not call for absolutism or for faith, which are signs of idealism in religion. What Neopagans accept and believe in depends on what makes sense to them, and that usually means what works for them. They are free to change as something more useful comes along, whether it be a tool, a ritual, or a belief. What works for one person, too, may not work for another. "Steal the best and hex the rest," as one Neopagan put it.[5]

A Second Chance, over Finality

Most Neopagan groups believe in reincarnation, which gives everyone several chances to succeed in life. In many of these religions, the self is seen as eternal, so a basic tenet of tragedy—that death is the end of the person—is denied.

Body and Not Just Spirit

Neopagan religions typically do not accept the dichotomy between body and spirit, and so they would not say that they celebrate body *over* spirit. But clearly they celebrate the physical side of life, as in eating, drinking, dancing, and sex. They see the body as sacred and beautiful, not sinful and ugly. Neopagan rituals are often performed "skyclad," in the nude. The great sacrament for Neopagans, "the Great Rite," is the symbolic enactment, or sometimes the physical act, of sexual intercourse.[6]

Playfulness over Seriousness

In a certain sense, all religions are serious—they care about what is central or sacred in their tradition. But in some religions, seriousness has become uniform solemnity. This is not the case in Neopaganism, which allows for considerable playfulness. When Neopagans meet in large groups for extended periods, they call their gathering a "festival." Revelry and mirth are a big part of such occasions. Laughter and joy are kinds of pleasure, and "all acts of love and pleasure are my ritual," as one rite, The Charge of the Goddess, expresses it. Seeing the humor in life is part of this festive attitude. As one Neopagan teacher put it, "The gods don't watch TV. We [humans] are a much better sit-com."

Our contrast of the comic and tragic visions in chapters 4 and 5 covered their social psychology as well as in their individual psychology. Here Neopaganism comes out on the comic side of all eight features we examined.

Anti-Heroism Instead of Heroism

Unlike the heroic vision, which celebrates idealized, larger-than-life individuals, the comic vision is concerned with ordinary people, warts and all. Most Neopagans are pro-comic on this score, acknowledging their limitations and shortcomings. The purpose of their magic is to heal their many human frailties.

Pacifism over Militarism

Because Neopagans are tolerant of the beliefs and practices of others, there are few principles to fight over. They reject harming others for one's own gain, and forcing one's ideas on others. Simply put, their motto is "Live and let live." Neopagans do try to overcome their own persecution by other groups, but they do that through education rather than violence.

Forgiveness Instead of Vengeance

Allowing for human frailties, Neopagans are relatively willing to forgive. Just as everyone gets another chance through reincarnation, everyone should be willing to give others a second chance.

Equality Rather Than Hierarchy

Much like the early Protestants, Neopagans reject hierarchical power and politics in religion. Instead they teach the equality of all. There are respected elders and teachers, but they are accepted by consensus rather than formally appointed. New members often go through initiation ceremonies and training, but that is done with little formal organization. The emphasis is on learning rather than on who has power and who lacks power.

More Sexual Equality

Unlike patriarchal religions, Neopagan religions either treat males and females equally, or in a few cases, emphasize the "goddess" as a corrective to millennia of patriarchal religions. Many leadership positions are held by women. Homosexuality is not disfavored.

Questioning of Authority and Tradition

With their egalitarianism, libertarianism, and acceptance of diverse beliefs and practices, Neopagans do not have authorities and traditions in the way traditional religions do. There are some roles, beliefs, and rituals that become systematic, but they can be changed when they no longer work for the group.

Situation Ethics Rather Than Rules

Neopaganism, like other new religions of the self, emphasizes the personal liberty of everyone, as we saw in the Wiccan Rede: "And it harms no one, do what you will." And so it values pluralism and tolerance. Neopagan morality is not a rule-based moral code like those of traditional authoritarian religions, but a philosophy of "Live and let live." If they can be said to have rules at all, Neopagans seem to have but one: Do not harm innocent persons unnecessarily. And even that is not a commandment handed down by a god, but simply a reasonable way to live, especially given the Threefold Law of Retribution. With its lack of emphasis on rules and its emphasis on respect for other people, Neopagan morality is more like the Situation Ethics of 1960s Christianity than it is like the Ten Commandments.

Social Integration Rather Than Isolation

Neopagan religions are thoroughly social. The basic group is the coven or clan, numbering no more than a few dozen, and it is important that all get along with each other. Individual freedom is valued, as we have seen, but only to the extent that one person's actions do not harm the community. Most festivals are set up, for example, to allow children to run free, but if they are doing something dangerous to others or to themselves, any adult may and should correct them.

Of the twenty pro-comic features of religions, Neopaganism has nineteen. The one pro-comic feature in chapter 5 that is not prominent in Neopaganism is emotional disengagement. Neopaganism is a romantic movement, and as such emphasizes feelings. Being emotionally involved in a situation is seen as part of being fully alive in that situation. And so Neopaganism does not cultivate the emotional distance characteristic of the comic vision. If emotional disengagement were merely one of twenty equally important pro-comic features, then we might say that Neopaganism is 95 percent comic. But emotional disengagement seems to be more central to the comic vision than other pro-comic features. In fact, if there is any one part of the comic vision that seems most important for religions, it is emotional disengagement. In the next chapter we will see why.

Chapter 9

The Value of Humor in Religion

From the many contrasts I have made between the comic and the tragic visions, it is obvious that I favor the comic vision. Especially important in any worldview, I think, is keeping one's sense of humor through life's good moments and bad. In this final chapter I would like to articulate one last time the importance of humor to religion.

The general case for humor in religion cannot be based on any particular metaphysics or theology, for different religions have conflicting beliefs. But all religions meet certain human needs, most importantly, by showing us how to live a fulfilling life, and here the comic spirit has much to contribute to any religion, whatever its metaphysics or theology.

Peter Berger has argued that "A Christian understanding of human existence would reverse the common belief that tragedy is more profound than comedy. On the contrary, this Christian understanding would say it is comedy that gives us the more significant insights into the human condition."[1] I agree, but would add that even apart from Christian eschatology, the comic vision is more profound and insightful than the tragic. To understand how, we need to extend our observations about the nature of humor from chapter 3.

Humor versus Emotions

The psychologist Daniel Berlyne once said that anyone designing a human race without having seen the actual one,

147

might see no reason why it could not conduct all its business in deadly earnest. Similarly, we might think it possible to have a religion whose members were uniformly solemn. But in fact the human race is not humorless, and neither are the followers of any religion. The reason, I think, is that human life is so full of failure, disappointment, and suffering, that without humor it would be unbearable. Or as Nietzsche suggested, our species had to invent laughter to get through life.[2]

In chapter 3 we analyzed humor as the enjoyment of incongruity, and saw how enjoying incongruity involves emotional disengagement from incongruity. The central lesson of comedy is that hardships are much easier to take if we reduce our practical concern and adopt a less emotional stance toward them. The tragic vision, on the other hand, encourages practical concern and emotional engagement with hardship, and so it celebrates emotions like anger, fear, and sadness.

The emotions championed by the tragic vision and avoided by the comic vision are often called "negative," because they involve unhappy feelings. But they are usually negative in another way, too, by interfering with our reaching our goals and living fulfilling lives. To understand this point, we need to say something about the role of emotions in human life.

Unlike humor, emotions are not unique to human beings but evolved early in mammals, as the limbic system of the brain developed. Emotions had survival value for animals because they prompted adaptive behavior in situations such as danger and loss. Moderate fear, for example, energizes an animal to run away, and thus escape danger. Epinephrine (adrenaline), the hormone in fear, makes the animal more alert, increases its strength, halts its digestion, and in other ways equips it to run away or defend itself. Intense fear or terror can be useful in situations of overwhelming danger. The animal "freezes," and thus may escape notice by the predator; or it "plays dead," which may stop the predator from attacking it. In anger, there is a release of blood sugar, giving the animal a burst of strength and stamina, to fight better and longer. Sadness, which in humans usually attends injury or the loss of something valuable, probably originated in the self-protective reactions of the lower animals to injury and illness. They immobilize the affected part of the body and reduce their overall movement; that reduces the chances of aggravating the injury, conserves energy, and facilitates healing. The negative feeling tone of sadness serves as negative reinforcement, motivating the animal to prevent a recurrence of a similar situation.

Humans inherited these and other emotions as part of their mammalian heritage, and in the early days, when human life was full of physical conflict, they served us well. Fear energized us to escape danger or defend ourselves, and anger to defend ourselves or attack enemies. Sadness got us to slow down, to recover from injury or loss, and pity got us to come to each other's aid. But today, when our lives are no longer based on hunting and fighting, these emotions are often counterproductive. Indeed, "stress" is our modern name for the emotions of fear and anger as they interfere with our lives. Consider the fear ranked number one on most surveys, the fear of public speaking. When humans lived as hunter-gatherers, it was adaptive for them to get scared when dozens of pairs of eyes were focused on them, for that usually occurred only when they were about to be attacked. We have inherited this reaction, and so when we get up to speak in front of an audience, no matter how friendly we know them to be, our bodies may react as those of our distant ancestors reacted to standing in an open space being stared at by hundreds of eyes. Similarly, anger was useful when we had to fight enemies and wild animals. In most situations today, however, responding to a problem with anger simply adds a second problem. Sadness, too, can be useful in getting us to slow down and withdraw from activity, but when it goes on for long, it is no longer useful.

The emotions celebrated in the tragic vision involve evolutionarily ancient reactions that often make our problems worse. Humor, on the other hand, is an evolutionarily new response not found in the lower animals. It is even centered in a different area of the brain, the neocortex, rather than in the more primitive limbic system.

Responding to problems with humor, I have suggested several times, is often better than reacting with tragic emotions. In laughing at a situation, we keep our cool: instead of being locked into a practical and personal perspective, we can see things in the big picture and from other people's perspectives. In this way, we can act rationally, as humans instead of as animals.

We can even use humor to block emotions, as when we joke with people who are getting scared, angry, or sad. A number of psychiatric techniques, in fact, take advantage of the opposition between humor and emotions.[3] In an exercise used to overcome chronic anxiety, for example, patients are told to schedule a five-minute period each day in which to feel as anxious as they can. When the alarm clock rings and they try to feel anxious, they feel silly instead and laugh, thus breaking the hold of their habitual anxiety.

While the major religions have seldom advocated humor as a way to block tragic emotions, most of them recognize the potential harmfulness of fear, anger, and sadness. Most, in fact, see it as one of their functions to help people overcome fear and sadness, and most condemn anger for fostering self-absorption and undermining social life. Religions as different as Buddhism and Christianity try to eliminate these emotions, Buddhism through nonattachment, Christianity through seeing all events from the perspective of Jesus. These religions do encourage sensitivity to other people's problems—compassion is a central virtue in both—but what is encouraged is helping people, not stewing in feelings of pity.

Comic Virtues

Since humor blocks tragic emotions, and since most religions treat the elimination of these emotions as virtuous, we should look for a connection between humor and virtue. I will argue that humor not only supports several virtues, but is itself a virtue.[4]

In the oldest and broadest sense of the word, a virtue is some excellence or power. The Greeks spoke of moral virtues, as we do, but also of intellectual virtues like wisdom. It is useful to consider the connection between humor and intellectual virtues before considering humor and moral virtues, because with humor, intellectual and moral virtues are closely linked.

In the comic frame of mind, we get out of our mental ruts to think flexibly. New perspectives and unusual connections between ideas are sought out; divergent thinking, imagination, and other forms of creativity are encouraged. The comic mind is always ready to consider another possible perspective. In this way, comic thinking fosters objectivity and rationality. We break free of thinking in the here and the now and the real and the practical. Instead of seeing things only from our own personal perspective, we can see them in the big picture. Reinhold Niebuhr said that "Humour is a proof of the capacity of the self to gain a vantage point from which it is able to look at itself. The sense of humour is thus a by-product of self-transcendence."[5] Indeed, perhaps the easiest way to tell whether people are capable of seeing themselves objectively is to find out whether they can laugh at themselves.

Humor also fosters critical thinking, another intellectual virtue. The comic mind looks for incongruity, especially between what is and what ought to be. The person with a sharp comic eye sees the discrepancies between what people say and what they do, for example, and more generally, sees everyone's feet of clay. A good sense of humor is thus protection against demagoguery and other harmful kinds of idealism; that is why iconoclasm is so often expressed with humor.

The critical spirit of humor is especially important in religion, where there is always a danger of zealotry, especially a danger of conferring transcendent value upon one's own limited ideas and interests. As Conrad Hyers said, laughter is "the lighthearted appendix to any 'ultimate and unconditional concern' that preserves it from absolutism."[6] With a sense of humor, we are unlikely to mistake our own sketchy and perhaps incorrect understanding of the transcendent for the transcendent itself. Humor's blocking of emotions is important here, too, for zealotry is driven by emotions. Those who burn books, or even burn heretics, are usually in the grip of pride and self-righteousness, which laughter would quickly dispel.

These intellectual virtues promoted by humor have obvious connections with moral virtues. Most fundamentally, the abstract thinking required for humor, the transcending of one's own interests and feelings, is the same kind of thinking required for moral reasoning. Persons locked into their own personal perspectives would be incapable of both humor and the moral point of view.

Humor's openness to fresh perspectives is also morally important, because it promotes tolerance of differences among people. Comedy's vast assortment of different human types—its courtesans and queens, its saints and scoundrels—can serve as a model for what we today call diversity.

A number of traditional virtues are fostered by humor. One is humility. "We are rather insignificant little bundles of energy and vitality in a vast organization of life," Reinhold Niebuhr wrote. "But we pretend that we are the very center of this organization. This pretension is ludicrous."[7] Religious people with a good sense of humor are unlikely to overrate their own importance or treat their own perspective on the transcendent as if it were Ultimate Truth.

Because a good sense of humor allows us to see ourselves and our projects in the big picture, too, it fosters the virtue of patience, with our own and other people's weaknesses and mistakes. That is why forgiveness, virtually absent from tragedy, is common in comedy. Because those with the comic vision understand that error and weakness are built into the human condition, they tend to be magnanimous and flexible rather than petty and rigid. In situations of conflict, they can see things from other people's perspectives, and so they can cooperate. The opposite of patience is anger, which, as we have said, most religions condemn.

Even when other people are clearly in the wrong, humor can help by giving the other person a graceful way out. When Barry Goldwater was an Arizona senator in the 1960s, he applied for membership in the Phoenix County Club. But because his father was Jewish, they rejected him. Goldwater telephoned the president of the country club to ask, "Since

I'm only half-Jewish, can I join if I just play nine holes?" The man laughed and let Goldwater into the club.

Beyond patience and magnanimity, humor can foster and express courage. When Winston Churchill went on BBC radio to tell the British people that Italy had entered World War II, for example, he put it this way, "Mussolini has announced that Italy is joining the war on the side of the Germans. I think that's only fair—we had to take them last time." During the Blitz in London, many shops had signs that said "Open as usual." After a particularly awful night of bombing, one shop with its windows blown out and its roof badly burned, sported the sign "More open than usual."

The most general benefit of humor is that it gives us a healthy attitude toward all the shortcomings and disorder built into the human condition. As Conrad Hyers said, "Comedy readily comes to terms with the arbitrariness of life, and with the muddiness of experience . . . by accepting this state of affairs as essential to the adventure itself."[8] The comic vision of life has often been criticized as frivolous and escapist. I would argue the opposite: that given the human condition, it is the most realistic vision we have. Indeed, a good sense of humor is very similar to the hard-headed virtue of wisdom. Niebuhr linked the two this way:

> To meet the disappointments and frustrations of life, the irrationalities and contingencies with laughter, is a high form of wisdom. Such laughter does not obscure or defy the dark irrationality. It merely yields to it without too much emotion or friction. A humorous acceptance of fate is really the expression of a high form of self-detachment.[9]

With humor, as with wisdom, we see things as part of the big picture, and we think for ourselves. We can debunk harmful visions of life like the ancient "Life is war" paradigm, and the current "Life is work" paradigm. Most importantly, we can gauge the relative importance of things. A fulfilled life is a balancing act, or better, a number of balancing acts, as Aristotle suggested with his idea that virtue is a mean. We need to balance hope with realism. We need a positive attitude toward ourselves and others without being Pollyannas. We need to balance the future with the present, looking ahead but avoiding an otherworldliness that trivializes today. With a good sense of humor, we can achieve this balance. We acknowledge our own and each other's value, as we smile at our foibles. We have ideals, but as we pursue them, we realize that in this life we can only approach ideals. We are confident, often enthusiastic, but are not crushed when we do not reach perfection. As the psychologist Penjon said early in this century, a sense of humor "frees us from vanity, on the one hand, and from pessimism, on the other, by keeping us larger than what we do and greater than what can happen to us."[10]

Humor, I conclude, not only fosters virtues, but is best seen as itself a virtue; and like wisdom, it is an intellectual and moral excellence of a high order. And any religion purporting to show people how to live needs to take it seriously.

Notes

Introduction

1. J. William Whedbee, "The Comedy of Job," *Semeia* 7 (1977): 1–39. Francis Landy, "Are We in the Place of Averroes?" *Semeia* 32 (1984): 133.

2. W. H. Auden, "The Christian Tragic Hero," *New York Times Book Review*, December 16, 1945, sect. 7, pp. 1, 21.

3. Roy Battenhouse, "Shakespearean Tragedy: A Christian Interpretation," in Nathan A. Scott, ed., *The Tragic Vision and the Christian Faith* (New York: Association Press, 1957), pp. 56–98.

4. Miguel de Unamuno, *The Tragic Sense of Life*, trans. J. E. Crawford Flitch (New York: Dover, 1954).

5. Karl Jaspers, *Tragedy Is Not Enough*, trans. Reich, Moore, and Deutsch (Hamden, Connecticut: Archon Books, 1969), p. 38.

6. George Skinner, *The Death of Tragedy* (New York: Hill and Wang, 1963), pp. 331–32.

7. D. D. Raphael, *The Paradox of Tragedy* (Bloomington: Indiana University Press, 1960), chap. 2.

8. Soren Kierkegaard, *Journals and Papers*, ed. and trans. Howard Hong and Edna Hong (Bloomington: Indiana University Press, 1970), Entries 1681–1682.

9. Reinhold Niebuhr, "Humour and Faith," in M. Conrad Hyers, ed., *Holy Laughter: Essays on Religion in the Comic Perspective* (New York: Seabury Press, 1969), pp. 134–49.

10. John Wheelock, "A True Poem Is a Way of Knowing," *New York Times Book Review*, May 23, 1954, p. 27.

11. Nathan A. Scott, "The Bias of Comedy and the Narrow Escape into Faith," in Hyers, *Holy Laughter*, chap. 3.

Chapter 1. Some Basic Connections

1. M. Conrad Hyers, "The Dialectic of the Sacred and the Comic," in M. Conrad Hyers, ed., *Holy Laughter: Essays on Religion in the Comic Perspective* (New York: Seabury Press, 1969), p. 232.

2. Reinhold Niebuhr, "Humour and Faith," in Hyers, *Holy Laughter*, p. 145.

3. R. H. Blyth, "Zen Humour," in Hyers, *Holy Laughter*, pp. 204–05.

4. Walter Kerr, *Tragedy and Comedy* (New York: Simon and Schuster, 1967), p. 189.

Chapter 2. The Nature of Tragedy

1. Quoted in Walter Kerr, *Tragedy and Comedy* (New York: Simon and Schuster, 1967), p. 93.

2. Aristotle, *Poetics*, in *Basic Works of Aristotle*, trans. Richard McKeon (New York: Random House, 1941), chap. 13.

3. Ibid.

4. A. C. Bradley, *Oxford Lectures on Poetry* (London: Macmillan, 1950), p. 91.

5. Nicolas Berdiaev, *The Destiny of Man*, trans. N. Duddington (London: Geoffrey Bles, 1948), pp. 18, 84.

6. See Jenefer Robinson, "*L'Éducation sentimentale*," *Australasian Journal of Philosophy*, 73 (1995). 212–226.

Chapter 3. The Nature of Comedy

1. J. Cheryl Exum and J. William Whedbee, "Isaac, Samson, and Saul: Reflections on the Comic and Tragic Visions," *Semeia* 32 (1984). 5–40. See Northrup Frye, "The Mythos of Spring," in Robert

Corrigan, ed., *Comedy: Meaning and Form* (Scranton, Pa.: Chandler, 1965).

2. Nathan A. Scott, "The Bias of Comedy and the Narrow Escape into Faith," in M. Conrad Hyers, ed., *Holy Laughter: Essays on Religion in the Comic Perspective* (New York: Seabury Press, 1969), p. 62.

3. See John Morreall, *Taking Laughter Seriously* (Albany: State University of New York Press, 1983), chaps. 3, 5, 6.

4. Peter Berger, "Christian Faith and the Social Comedy," in Hyers, *Holy Laughter*, chap. 7.

5. See John Morreall, ed., *The Philosophy of Laughter and Humor* (Albany: State University of New York Press, 1987), chapter 11.

6. For more detailed replies to historical objections to humor, see John Morreall, "The Rejection of Humor in Western Thought," *Philosophy East and West* 39 (1989): 243–65.

7. See John Morreall, "Enjoying Incongruity," *Humor: International Journal of Humor Research* 2 (1989): 1–18.

8. See Henri Bergson, *Laughter*, trans. Cloudesley Brereton and Kenneth Rothwell, in Morreall, *The Philosophy of Laughter and Humor*, p. 118.

9. See *Comic Epitaphs*, no author (Mt. Vernon: Peter Pauper Press, 1957).

10. Walter Kerr, *Tragedy and Comedy*, (New York: Simon and Schuster, 1967), pp. 78–79.

Chapter 4. The Tragic Vision versus The Comic Vision

1. Suzanne Langer, *Feeling and Form* (New York: Scribner, 1953), pp. 333, 327.

2. Walter Kerr shows how many of the endings of Shakespeare's comedies are not happy for the characters involved, in his *Tragedy and Comedy* (New York: Simon & Schuster, 1967), pp. 57–63.

3. George Aichele, *Theology as Comedy* (Lanham, Md.: University Press of America, 1980), p. 26. See Langer, *Feeling and Form*, p. 349.

4. See John Morreall, "Enjoying Incongruity," *Humor: International Journal of Humor Research* 2 (1989): 1–18. See also John Morreall, "Funny Ha-Ha, Funny Strange, and Other Reactions to Incongruity," in John Morreall, ed., *The Philosophy of Laughter and Humor* (Albany: State University of New York Press, 1987), chap. 20.

5. See William F. Lynch, "The Humanity of Comedy," in M. Conrad Hyers, ed., *Holy Laughter: Essays on Religion in the Comic Perspective* (New York: Seabury Press, 1969), pp. 40–41.

6. See Victor Raskin, *Semantic Mechanisms of Humor* (Synthese Language Library 24) (Dordrecht: D. Reidel, 1985).

7. Harvey Cox, *The Feast of Fools: A Theological Essay on Festivity and Fantasy* (Cambridge: Harvard University Press, 1969), p. 155.

8. Conrad Hyers, *And God Created Laughter: The Bible as Divine Comedy* (Atlanta: John Knox Press, 1987), pp. 116–17.

9. Henry Alonzo Myers, *Tragedy: A View of Life* (Ithaca: Cornell University Press, 1956), p. 45.

10. Erma Bombeck, "Me Have Cancer?" *Redbook*, October 1992.

11. Walter Kerr, *Tragedy and Comedy* (New York: Simon and Schuster, 1967), p. 139.

12. Langer, *Feeling and Form*, p. 333.

13. Henri Bergson, *Laughter*, trans. Cloudesley Brereton and Kenneth Rothwell, in Morreall, *The Philosophy of Laughter and Humor*, pp. 120–26.

14. Kerr, *Tragedy and Comedy*, p. 164.

15. Christopher Fry, *A Phoenix Too Frequent*, in *Selected Plays* (New York: Oxford University Press, 1985), p. 95.

16. Aristophanes, *Four Plays*, trans. John Hookham Frere (London: Oxford University Press, 1907), p. 8.

17. Nathan A. Scott, "The Bias of Comedy and the Narrow Escape into Faith," in Hyers, *Holy Laughter*, p. 57.

18. Kerr, *Tragedy and Comedy*, p. 174.

19. Ibid., p. 182.

Chapter 5. The Tragic and the Comic Visions in Religions

1. Conrad Hyers, *And God Created Laughter: The Bible as Divine Comedy* (Atlanta: John Knox, 1987), chap. 7.

2. Reinhold Niebuhr, "Humour and Faith," in M. Conrad Hyers, ed., *Holy Laughter: Essays on Religion in the Comic Perspective* (New York: Seabury Press, 1969), p. 139.

3. Peter Berger, "Christian Faith and the Social Comedy," in Hyers, *Holy Laughter*, p. 129.

4. Conrad Hyers, *And God Created Laughter*, p. 114.

5. Walter Kerr, *Tragedy and Comedy* (New York: Simon & Schuster, 1967), p. 264.

Chapter 6. Eastern Religions

1. Swami Prabhavananda, *Vedic Religion and Philosophy* (Mylapore: Sri Ramakrishna Math Press, n.d.), pp. 9–10.

2. D. S. Sarma, *Essence of Hinduism* (Bombay: Bharatiya Vidya Bhavan, 1988), p. 59.

3. Henri Bergson, *Laughter*, trans. Cloudesley Brereton and Kenneth Rothwell, in John Morreall, ed., *The Philosophy of Laughter and Humor* (Albany: State University of New York Press, 1987), p. 118.

4. Philip Kapleau, *The Three Pillars of Zen* (Boston: Beacon, 1965), p. 208.

5. Sigmund Freud, "Humor," in *Collected Papers*, vol. 5 (New York: Basic Books, 1959).

6. Edward Conze, *Buddhist Meditation* (New York: Harper Torchbooks, 1969), pp. 100–103.

7. Kapleau, *The Three Pillars of Zen*, p. 205.

8. These and similar examples can be found in Conrad Hyers, *The Laughing Buddha: Zen and the Comic Spirit* (Durango, Colo.: Longwood Academic, 1991), especially chap. 4.

9. Lao Tzu, *Tao Teh King*, 2d ed., trans. Archie Bahm (Albuquerque, N. Mex.: World Books, 1986), p. 15.

10. D. C. Lau, trans., *The Mencius* (London: Penguin, 1983), 6b.2.

11. D. C. Lau, trans., *The Analects* (London: Penguin, 1979), A 1.8.

12. Translations of the *Tao Te Ching* are from Archie Bahm, *Tao Teh King*, 2nd ed. (Albuquerque, N. Mex.: World Books, 1986).

13. *Chuang Tzu*, book 7, trans. James Legge, in Robert E. Van Voorst, ed., *Anthology of World Scriptures* (Belmont, Calif.: Wadsworth, 1994), p. 176.

Chapter 7. Western Religions

1. Indeed, she laughs too, and they name their son Isaac—laughter!

2. All translations of the *Book of Job* are from Stephen Mitchell, *The Book of Job* (New York: HarperCollins, 1992).

3. Ibid., p. xvii.

4. Conrad Hyers, *And God Created Laughter: The Bible as Divine Comedy* (Atlanta: John Knox Press, 1987), chap. 7.

5. J. Cheryl Exum and J. William Whedbee, "Isaac, Samson, and Saul: Reflections on the Comic and Tragic Visions," *Semeia* 32 (1984): 9–19.

6. J. William Whedbee, "The Comedy of Job," *Semeia* 7 (1977): 1–39.

7. Exum and Whedbee, "Isaac, Samson, and Saul," *Semeia* 32 (1984): 10, emphasis in original.

8. Ibid., 19.

9. Ibid., 18. Cf. ibid., 16: "As passive victim Isaac is one more often laughed at or over rather than one who laughs himself or laughs with others."

10. Francis Landy, "Are We in the Place of Averroes?" *Semeia* 32 (1984): 139.

11. Exum and Whedbee, "Isaac, Samson, and Saul," *Semeia* 32 (1984): 11.

12. Landy, "Are We in the Place of Averroes?" *Semeia* 32 (1984): 139.

13. See also Matt. 5:27–30, Matt. 9:42–49, Matt. 10:28, Matt. 11:23–24, Matt. 13: 24–30, Matt. 13:36–43, Matt. 18:8–9, Mark 9:42-49, Luke 10:15, Luke 12:5, Luke 16:19-31.

14. Elton Trublood, *The Humor of Christ* (New York: Harper and Row, 1964).

15. See Elaine Pagels, *Adam, Eve, and the Serpent* (New York: Random House, 1988), chaps. 5-6.

16. Matt. 5:38–48, Rom. 12:14, 17–21.

17. See John Driver, *How Christians Made Peace with War* (Scottdale, Pa.: Herald Press, 1988).

18. John Calvin, *Compendium of the Institutes of the Christian Religion*, ed. Hugh Kerr (Philadelphia: Westminster, 1964), book II.i. 6–7.

19. Ibid. II.ii. 15.

20. Ibid. II.iii. 4.

21. Ibid. III.xxiv. 15–16.

22. Harvey Cox, *The Feast of Fools* (Cambridge: Harvard University Press, 1969), p. 156.

23. Karl Barth, *Church Dogmatics* (Edinburgh: T & T Clark, 1961), p. 262ff.

24. St. John Chrysostom, *On the Priesthood; Ascetic Treatises; Select Homilies and Letters; Homilies on the Statues*, vol. 9 of *A Select Library of the Nicene and Post-Nicene Fathers of the Christian Church*, ed. Philip Schaff (New York: The Christian Literature Co., 1889), p. 442.

25. Cox, *The Feast of Fools*, pp. 140–41.

26. Ibid., p. 140.

27. See Marlow Hotchkiss, "Sunday Masks and Pagan Faces," *Religious Theatre* 2 (1965): 59–76.

28. Wolfgang F. Zucker, "The Clown as the Lord of Disorder," in M. Conrad Hyers, ed., *Holy Laughter: Essays on Religion in the Comic Perspective* (New York: Seabury Press, 1969), p. 84; Cox, *The Feast of Fools*, p. 3.

29. Cox, *The Feast of Fools*, p. 142.

30. Elton Trueblood, "The Humor of Christ," in Hyers, *Holy Laughter*, p. 182.

31. Northrup Frye, "The Argument of Comedy," in *Theories of Comedy*, ed. Paul Lauter (Garden City, N.Y.: Doubleday); reprinted from *English Institute Essays* (New York: Columbia University Press, 1948), p. 455.

32. Reinhold Niebuhr, "Humour and Faith," in Hyers, *Holy Laughter*, p. 141.

33. M. Conrad Hyers, "The Dialectic of the Sacred and the Comic," in Hyers, *Holy Laughter*, p. 227.

34. Niebuhr, "Humour and Faith," in Hyers, *Holy Laughter*, p. 135.

35. Cox, *The Feast of Fools*, p. 47.

36. Ibid., p. 139.

Chapter 8. New Religions

1. Peter Clarke, "Beyond Death: The Case of New Religions," in Dan Cohn-Sherbok and Christopher Lewis, eds., *Beyond Death* (New York: St. Martin's, 1995), p. 127.

2. For most of the following information about American Neopaganism, I am indebted to Scott Russell.

3. Janet Farrar and Stewart Farrar, *The Witches Way* (New York: Magickal Childe, 1984), p. 135.

4. Janet Farrar and Stewart Farrar, *Eight Sabbats for Witches* (New York: Magickal Childe, 1981), p. 39.

5. Ron Parshley is a Witan Elder in the Tampa Bay Community.

6. Janet Farrar and Stewart Farrar, *The Life and Times of a Modern Witch* (Custer, Wash.: Phoenix, 1987), pp. 74–93.

Chapter 9. The Value of Humor in Religion

1. Peter L. Berger, "Christian Faith and the Social Comedy," in M. Conrad Hyers, ed., *Holy Laughter: Essays on Religion in the Comic Perspective* (New York: Seabury Press, 1969), p. 128.

2. For a fuller treatment of the opposition between humor and emotions, see John Morreall, "Humor and Emotion," in John Morreall, ed., *The Philosophy of Laughter and Humor* (Albany: State University of New York Press, 1987), pp. 212–24.

3. See Allen Fay, *Making Things Better by Making Them Worse* (New York: Hawthorn, 1978); William F. Fry, M.D., and Waleed Salameh, ed., *Handbook of Humor and Psychotherapy: Advances in the Clinical Uses of Humor* (Sarasota, Fla.: Professional Resource Exchange, 1987).

4. See Robert C. Roberts, "Humor and the Virtues," *Inquiry* 31 (1988): 127–49.

5. Reinhold Niebuhr, "Humour and Faith," in Hyers, *Holy Laughter*, p. 140.

6. M. Conrad Hyers, "The Dialectic of the Sacred and the Comic," in Hyers, *Holy Laughter*, p. 221.

7. Niebuhr, "Humour and Faith," in Hyers, *Holy Laughter*, p. 141.

8. Conrad Hyers, *The Spirituality of Comedy: Comic Heroism in a Tragic World* (New Brunswick, N.J.: Transaction, 1996), p. 175.

9. Niebuhr, "Humour and Faith," in Hyers, *Holy Laughter*, p. 145.

10. Quoted in Max Eastman, *The Sense of Humor* (New York: Scribner's, 1921), p. 188.

Bibliography

Biblical quotations except from *The Book of Job* are from *The New English Bible*. Oxford and Cambridge: Oxford University Press and Cambridge University Press, 1970. Quotations from *The Book of Job* are from the translation of Stephen Mitchell.

Aichele, George. *Theology as Comedy*. Lanham, Md.: University Press of America, 1980.

Aristotle. *Poetics*. In Richard McKeon, trans., *Basic Works of Aristotle*. New York: Random House, 1941.

Auden, W. H. "The Christian Tragic Hero." *New York Times Book Review*, December 16, 1945, sect. 7, pp. 1, 21.

Barth, Karl. *Church Dogmatics*. Edinburgh: T & T Clark, 1961.

Battenhouse, Roy. "Shakespearean Tragedy: A Christian Interpretation." In Nathan A. Scott, ed., *The Tragic Vision and the Christian Faith*. New York: Association Press, 1957, pp. 56–98.

Berdiaev, Nicolas. *The Destiny of Man*. Trans. N. Duddington. London: Geoffrey Bles, 1948.

Berger, Peter. "Christian Faith and the Social Comedy." In M. Conrad Hyers, ed., *Holy Laughter: Essays on Religion in the Comic Perspective*. New York: Seabury Press, 1969.

———. *Redeeming Laughter: An Essay on the Experience of the Comic.* New York: Aldine de Gruyter, 1997.

Bergson, Henri. *Laughter.* Trans. by Cloudesley Brereton and Kenneth Rothwell. In Wylie Sypher, ed., *Comedy.* Garden City, N.Y.: Doubleday Anchor, 1956.

Blyth, R. H. "Zen Humour." In M. Conrad Hyers, ed., *Holy Laughter: Essays on Religion in the Comic Perspective.* New York: Seabury Press, 1969.

Bombeck, Erma. "Me Have Cancer?" *Redbook,* October 1992.

Bradley, A. C. *Oxford Lectures on Poetry.* London: Macmillan, 1950.

Buckley, George. *The Wit and Wisdom of Jesus.* Battle Creek, Mich.: Ellis, 1901.

Calvin, John. *Compendium of the Institutes of the Christian Religion,* ed. Hugh Kerr. Philadelphia: Westminster, 1964.

Chrysostom, John. *On the Priesthood; Ascetic Treatises; Select Homilies and Letters; Homilies on the Statues,* vol. 9 of *A Select Library of the Nicene and Post-Nicene Fathers of the Christian Church,* ed. Philip Schaff. New York: The Christian Literature Co., 1889.

Conze, Edward. *Buddhist Meditation.* New York: Harper Torchbooks, 1969.

Cox, Harvey. *The Feast of Fools: A Theological Essay on Festivity and Fantasy.* Cambridge: Harvard University Press, 1969.

Croissan, Dominic. *Raid on the Articulate: Comic Eschatology in Jesus and Borges.* New York: Harper & Row, 1976.

Driver, John. *How Christians Made Peace with War.* Scottdale, Pa.: Herald Press, 1988.

Exum, J. Cheryl. *Tragedy and Biblical Narrative.* Cambridge: Cambridge University Press, 1992.

Exum, J. Cheryl, and Whedbee, J. "Isaac, Samson, and Saul: Reflections on the Comic and Tragic Visions," *Semeia* 32 (1984): 5–40.

Farley, Wendy. *Tragic Vision and Divine Compassion: A Contemporary Theodicy.* Louisville: Westminster/John Knox Press, 1990.

Freud, Sigmund. "Humor." In *Collected Papers*, vol. 5. New York: Basic Books, 1959.

Fry, William, and Salameh, Waleed, eds. *Handbook of Humor and Psychotherapy: Advances in the Clinical Uses of Humor.* Sarasota, Fla.: Professional Resource Exchange, 1987.

Frye, Northrup. "The Argument of Comedy." In *Theories of Comedy*, ed. Paul Lauter. Garden City, N.Y.: Doubleday. Reprinted from *English Institute Essays.* New York: Columbia University Press, 1948.

———. "The Mythos of Spring." In Robert Corrigan, ed., *Comedy: Meaning and Form.* Scranton, Pa.: Chandler, 1965.

Grassi, Joseph. *God Makes Me Laugh: A New Approach to Luke.* Collegeville, Minn.: Liturgical Press, 1986.

Hamilton, Edith. "Comedy," *Theatre Arts Monthly*, 11 (1927): 503–12.

Hotchkiss, Marlow. "Sunday Masks and Pagan Faces," *Religious Theatre* 2 (1965): 59–76.

Hunt, Barbara. *The Paradox of Christian Tragedy.* Troy, N.Y.: Whitston, 1985.

Hyers, Conrad M. *And God Created Laughter: The Bible as Divine Comedy.* Atlanta: John Knox Press, 1987.

———. *The Laughing Buddha: Zen and the Comic Spirit.* Durango, Colo.: Longwood Academic, 1991.

———. *The Spirituality of Comedy: Comic Heroism in a Tragic World.* New Brunswick, N.J.: Transaction, 1996.

———. "The Dialectic of the Sacred and the Comic." In M. Conrad Hyers, ed., *Holy Laughter: Essays on Religion in the Comic Perspective.* New York: Seabury Press, 1969.

Jaspers, Karl. *Tragedy Is Not Enough,* trans. Reich, Moore, and Deutsch. Hamden, Conn.: Archon Books, 1969.

Kapleau, Philip. *The Three Pillars of Zen.* Boston: Beacon, 1965.

Kerr, Walter. *Tragedy and Comedy.* New York: Simon & Schuster, 1967.

Kierkegaard, Soren. *Journals and Papers,* ed. and trans. by Howard Hong and Edna Hong. Bloomington: Indiana University Press, 1970.

Krieger, Murray. *The Tragic Vision.* New York: Holt, Rinehart and Winston, 1960.

Landy, Francis. "Are We in the Place of Averroes?" *Semeia* 32 (1984): 131–48.

Langer, Suzanne. *Feeling and Form.* New York: Scribner, 1953.

Lao Tzu. *Tao Teh King,* 2d ed. trans. Archie Bahm. Albuquerque, N. Mex.: World Books, 1986.

Lauter, Paul, ed. *Theories of Comedy.* New York: Doubleday Anchor, 1969.

Legge, James, trans. *The Chinese Classics.* Oxford: Oxford University Press, 1893.

———, trans. *The Texts of Taoism, Sacred Books of the East,* vols. 39 and 40. Oxford: Oxford University Press, 1891.

Lynch, William F. "The Humanity of Comedy." In M. Conrad Hyers, ed., *Holy Laughter: Essays on Religion in the Comic Perspective*. New York: Seabury Press, 1969.

Mitchell, Stephen. *The Book of Job*. New York: Harper Collins, 1992.

Morreall, John. "The Comic and Tragic Visions of Life," *Humor: International Journal of Humor Research* 11 (1998): 333–55.

———. "Enjoying Incongruity," *Humor: International Journal of Humor Research* 2 (1989): 1–18.

———. "Funny Ha-Ha, Funny Strange, and Other Reactions to Incongruity." In John Morreall, ed., *The Philosophy of Laughter and Humor*. Albany: State University of New York Press, 1987.

———, ed. *The Philosophy of Laughter and Humor*. Albany: State University of New York Press, 1987.

———. "The Rejection of Humor in Western Thought." *Philosophy East and West* 39 (1989): 243–65.

———. *Taking Laughter Seriously*. Albany: State University of New York Press, 1983.

Myers, Henry Alonzo. *Tragedy: A View of Life*. Ithaca, N.Y.: Cornell University Press, 1956.

Niebuhr, Reinhold. "Humour and Faith." In M. Conrad Hyers, ed., *Holy Laughter: Essays on Religion in the Comic Perspective*. New York: Seabury Press, 1969.

Obayashi, Hiroshi, ed. *Death and Afterlife: Perspectives of World Religions*. Westport, Conn.: Greenwood, 1992.

Pagels, Elaine. *Adam, Eve, and the Serpent*. New York: Random House, 1988.

Prabhavananda, Swami. *Vedic Religion and Philosophy*. Mylapore: Sri Ramakrishna Math Press, n.d.

Raphael, D. D. *The Paradox of Tragedy*. Bloomington: Indiana University Press, 1960.

Raskin, Victor. *Semantic Mechanisms of Humor*. Synthese Language Library 24. Dordrecht: D. Reidel, 1985.

Robinson, Jenefer. "*L'Éducation sentimentale*," *Australasian Journal of Philosophy* 73 (1995): 212–26.

Samra, Cal, and Rose Samra. *Holy Humor*. Nashville, Tenn.: Thomas Nelson. 1997.

Sarma, D. S. *Essence of Hinduism*. Bombay: Bharatiya Vidya Bhavan, 1988.

Scott, Nathan A. "The Bias of Comedy and the Narrow Escape into Faith." In M. Conrad Hyers, ed., *Holy Laughter: Essays on Religion in the Comic Perspective*. New York: Seabury Press, 1969.

Skinner, George. *The Death of Tragedy*. New York: Hill and Wang, 1963.

Trueblood, Elton. *The Humor of Christ*. New York: Harper & Row, 1964.

———. "The Humor of Christ." in M. Conrad Hyers, ed., *Holy Laughter: Essays on Religion in the Comic Perspective*. New York: Seabury Press, 1969.

Unamuno, Miguel de. *The Tragic Sense of Life*, trans. J. E. Crawford Flitch. New York: Dover, 1954.

Van Voorst, Robert E., ed. *Anthology of World Scriptures*. Belmont, Calif.: Wadsworth, 1994.

Via, Dan O. *Kerygma and Comedy in the New Testament*. Philadelphia: Fortress, 1975.

Whedbee, J. William. "The Comedy of Job," *Semeia* 7 (1977): 1–39.

Wheelock, John. "A True Poem Is a Way of Knowing." *New York Times Book Review*, May 23, 1954, p. 27.

Willeford, William. *The Fool and His Sceptre: A Study in Clowns and Jesters and Their Audience.* Evanston, Ill.: Northwestern University Press, 1969.

Zucker, Wolfgang F. "The Clown as the Lord of Disorder." In M. Conrad Hyers, ed., *Holy Laughter: Essays on Religion in the Comic Perspective.* New York: Seabury Press, 1969.

Index